The Divorced Child

First published in 2010 by
PALGRAVE MACMILLAN®
in the United States—a division of St. Martin's Press LLC,
175 Fifth Avenue, New York, NY 10010.

Where this book is distributed in the UK, Europe and the rest of the
world, this is by Palgrave Macmillan, a division of Macmillan Publishers
Limited, registered in England, company number 785998, of Houndmills,
Basingstoke, Hampshire RG21 6XS.

Palgrave Macmillan is the global academic imprint of the above companies
and has companies and representatives throughout the world.

Palgrave® and Macmillan® are registered trademarks in the United States,
the United Kingdom, Europe and other countries.

ISBN: 978–0–230–61772–8

Library of Congress Cataloging-in-Publication Data is available from the
Library of Congress.

A catalogue record of the book is available from the British Library.

Design by Newgen Imaging Systems (P) Ltd., Chennai, India.

First edition: February 2010

10 9 8 7 6 5 4 3 2 1

Printed in the United States of America.

The Divorced C

Strengthening You
Family through the Fi
Three Years of Separat

Joseph Nowinski, Ph.D.

palgrave
macmillan

For Maggie—Living proof that what is written here is true
And for Becca and Greg

Contents

Introduction:
The Three Crucial Years

What Parents Need to
Know about Children and Divorce

You can do this!

If you are reading these words it is most likely because you are a parent and are either thinking about getting a divorce, are in the midst of one, or are dealing with its immediate aftermath.

There is no denying that that divorce represents a great challenge, for you as a divorcing parent as well as for your child or children. Divorce is one of those crises that affect virtually every aspect of a person's life. Yet, as challenging as it is, divorce in America has become commonplace. Here are a few vital statistics on divorce:

- Approximately 50 percent of American marriages end in divorce.
- Approximately 60 percent of *re*marriages end in divorce.
- Approximately 43 percent of marriages are remarriages for at least one of the parties.
- Approximately one million children will have newly separated or divorced parents *each year*.

Most people's fear in undergoing divorce is the effect it will have on the children. These fears may have had their origin in a time when divorce, contrary to the above statistics, was a rare event. Fifty years ago, children from divorced parents were commonly described as coming from "broken homes," and they had to live with the stigma that such a phrase implies. To compound matters, much of the early research on the effects of divorce reinforced the notion that all children were negatively affected, and for their entire lives.

There is no denying that, on the list of stressful life events, divorce ranks high. This book aims to show you how it is possible for you and your child not only to survive this crisis, but to emerge from it stronger and happier in the long run. You as a parent need to know that divorce does not have to result in permanent damage to the psyche of the child or children you care so much about. This is not wishful thinking, but a fact that is supported by research. The premise of this book is that it is possible for children to face this challenge successfully. In other words, *your child can emerge from the next three years a more resilient, self-confident individual.* Remember, this is your child's divorce as much as it is yours. You child is perfectly capable of surviving this upheaval, but will likely need some support and guidance along the way. This book will help you identify the potential pitfalls that lie ahead, and will be your guide you in keeping your child on that healthy developmental track.

Financial and Emotional Burdens

In the years immediately ahead, you and your child will most likely face many changes—including where you live and the kind of *lifestyle* you will lead. The majority of children of divorce must relocate or adjust to dividing their time between two households; sometimes both. Many have to change schools at least once. Their overall standard of living is apt to decline. According to the U.S. Census Bureau, 64 percent of married couples with children younger than 18 must rely on two incomes to make ends meet. When parents divorce, that same combined income has to support two households. Child support may help to cushion the financial blow to children of divorce, but it rarely eliminates it.

Your Parental Responsibilities

Your goal as a parent is *not* to prevent your child from ever experiencing a crisis. Although all parents have an instinctive desire to protect their children, life inevitably has its difficulties, and it is unrealistic to think that you can actually shield your child from ever facing one.

What you *do* want to do is show your child how to process problems and weather situations in ways that help him or her grow. In a word, you want to help your child become *resilient*. You will be learning a great deal about resilience in this book, and how you can help build this important aspect of your child's personality. Whether they realize it consciously or not, good parents are building resilience and self-confidence in their children all the time. They do this when they teach their children how to swim; they do it when they teach their children how to respond if approached by a stranger; and they do it when they conduct periodic fire drills in their homes. Finally, they are building resilience and self-confidence when they encourage and coach their children to set goals and persevere even in the face of obstacles along the way.

Another one of your parental responsibilities is to teach your child how to find and use his or her "voice." By this I mean teaching your child how to express his or her opinions, how to engage in healthy conflict, and how to stand up for what he or she believes in.

Divorce, like a house fire, is a crisis. How an individual comes through such a crisis depends, in large part, on how well prepared they are for it, and on how they are guided through it. To address this need, I have divided this book into sections that deal with various phases in the process. Taken together, they represent a "road map" of the critical developmental tasks that your child will face as he or she moves from toddlerhood through adolescence. Each section includes descriptions of the issues that most often come up for children in divorce, along with specific suggestions for what you can do if and when one of these issues does arise. Armed with this knowledge, you will be able to spot problems early on and intervene as needed to keep your child on a healthy developmental track. As long as she or he is on such a track, you have done your job.

Another goal for you as a parent is to maintain your own physical and emotional health so that you can be in a position to guide your child effectively. That's why this book, unlike other books on children and divorce, also includes a section for *you*. You will not be able to do your best at helping your child to cope with your divorce, and emerge a more resilient person for it, if you are compromised for one reason or another.

What We Now Know About Divorce

When divorce started to become a fact of modern life, much of the literature drew a gloomy picture about its effects on children. Usually the conclusions were based on studies with very small sample pools. More importantly, these studies failed to compare children of divorce to children from so-called intact families, to see what if any *differences* there were between these two groups. For example, are teenagers from divorced families any more moody than teens from two-parent homes?

Fortunately, in the intervening years, additional research on children and divorce has emerged. This includes studies that followed large groups of children over a period of years. For the reader who is interested, these studies are cited in the chapter notes at the end of the book. The data collected by these researchers was based on observational studies and interviews, as well as objective personality and academic achievement test scores. Moreover, the researchers were able to compare children whose parents divorced to children whose parents did not. This research has led to a much clearer and more focused picture of the effects of divorce on children.

The Impact on Children

One of your major fears about divorce no doubt is that it will leave permanent emotional scars on your child or on your children. You might fear that it will lower their self esteem, that they will feel unloved, that they will lose motivation to succeed in school, or that their idea of what it's like to have a family will be irrevocably stained. All of these fears are normal and expected.

Our society allocates many resources to understanding the legacy of family break-ups on its youngest and most vulnerable members. And most recently we have learned a lot about its real impact.

Although *three out of four* children of divorce will recover from any ill effects within three years, as many as *one out of four* will experience more serious social, academic, or psychological problems. If they occur, these problems will most likely rear their heads during the *first three years* that these children's parents are going through their divorce. If these problems are not addressed during this critical three-year window, they could have longstanding effects.

Three Crucial Years

Several researchers have followed large numbers of children over a long period of time, and have also compared those whose parents divorced to those whose parents did not. These children were assessed at regular intervals. What the researchers found is that, three years after separation or divorce, the divorced children were, as a group, more *similar* to children of intact families than different. In other words, divorce does *not* invariably lead to psychological, social, legal, or academic problems. At this three-year mark, the majority of children of divorce appear to have weathered the storm, psychologically speaking, and are no different from their non-divorced peers. At the same time, these regular assessments identified a minority—25 percent—of divorced children who were experiencing significant problems that would need to be addressed if these children were to get back on track, developmentally speaking.

Different Ages, Different Needs

During the three crucial years, divorce affects children of different ages in different ways. Toddlers and young children are developing differently and so will react differently to divorce than older children or adolescents. In order to ease a child's transition, parents need to understand the developmental pace of their children, to recognize early signs of trouble, and to know how to intervene.

What this Means for You

The above facts about children and divorce have some clear implications for you as a divorcing parent:

- You can take solace knowing that, if your child or children can successfully negotiate the first three crucial years following divorce, chances are they will be emerge healthy in the long run.
- You need to be vigilant for potential pitfalls and ready to act during the critical three years.
- Armed with a *developmental road map,* you can understand your child's emotions at the moment and anticipate what problems may come up in the future, and how you can intervene. The particular issues that may arise, and that you need to be vigilant for, will depend to some extent on your child's age.

- You need to pay attention to *yourself* as well as your children to ensure that you are in a position to monitor their development, identify any emerging problems early, and intervene effectively.
- Your challenge is *not* to insulate your child or children from stress, or to make sure that their lives do not change at all as a result of your divorce. Rather, your challenge is to make sure that your child or children stay a healthy developmental course. Children are not fragile, and those who stay on a healthy track are quite capable of coping for themselves. If anything, your child may emerge from your divorce as a stronger, self-confident individual.

How to Use this Book

This book is organized to help you guide your child safely through divorce.

Part One addresses issues that many if not all divorcing parents will need to face, sooner or later. These include how to explain divorce to your child, which will vary depending on your child's developmental level. Other issues that parents may need to face at some point are relocating children, working out shared parenting arrangements, introducing a new partner, and taking the first steps toward becoming a blended family. Each chapter includes specific advice and guidelines.

Part Two of the book asks you to consider the effect that separation and divorce may have on you. As parents our instinct is to prioritize our child; but we can best minister to our children's needs when ours are in order. As much as you may be concerned about your children, divorce can significantly impair parents' ability to function at their best. My goal is to help you be sure that you will be able to be "part of the solution"; in other words, be in a position to help your child successfully navigate through the next three years.

The last three parts of the book correspond to the three different developmental levels. Part Three discusses toddlers and young children (ages 1 to 5). Part Four deals with older children (ages 6 to 11). Part Five discusses preteens and teenagers (ages 11 to 18). Depending on the age of your child or children, you may want to turn your attention immediately to one of these sections, and the chapters therein. However, if you have a child who will be transitioning from one of these developmental stages to another over the course of the next three years, you should definitely familiarize yourself with the material that pertains to each stage. That way you will have a road map that can help you understand not only what your child is going right now, but what you can expect in the future. The material and advice in these chapters will be useful to all separating parents. However, it will be especially useful to separated parents who have negotiated a shared parenting agreement but who have had less hands-on parenting experience prior to their separation.

Part One

Child-Centered Divorce

Before we begin to sort out issues faced by divorced children at different stages of development, let us look at some issues that almost all divorcing parents will eventually need to deal with. Naturally, just how you as a divorcing parent will deal with each of these issues—for example, talking to your child about divorce—will differ depending on how old your child is. That said, these are all bridges that will have to be crossed sooner or later, so it makes sense to examine them at the outset.

Chapter 1
The Divorced Family

Divorce is not something that happens only to spouses. Whenever there are children involved, divorce is a family matter. It is vital that separated parents keep this in mind. It is not only their own lives that are going through an upheaval, but also their children's lives, as well as the lives of the extended family. Everyone must adjust to a new reality.

Children are not emotionally fragile to the extent that they are not capable of surviving a crisis such as divorce. As discussed earlier, most children do adjust and emerge from divorce emotionally, socially, and academically unscathed. A minority do not. This book aims to help you as a parent ensure that your child will be one of those who survives and thrives.

Robert and Julia

Robert was six and his sister Julia was eight when their mother and father told them that they were getting a divorce. As is typical of children this age, neither one cried. But that did not mean that all was necessarily okay on the inside.

Julia and Robert had an idea of what divorce meant. Julia's best friend Emily's parents had recently divorced. When asked about it Julia replied, "Emily's father moved out. He was hardly ever there anyway. Now I never see him." Asked how she thought Emily felt about her parents' divorce, Julia said, "She's sad. But she said she just doesn't think about it most of the time."

It was true that Emily did not think about her parents' divorce. At the same time, in that school year Emily was out "sick" fifteen days. In prior years she'd been out sick a maximum of three days. Moreover, her progress in reading and other academic subjects slid from near the top of her peer group to somewhere below average.

Although children are reticent to talk to their own parents about divorce, it is a mistake to think that they do not talk to one another about it. In a way this is understandable, since they are reluctant to offend or risk alienating that parent, by expressing anger, for example.

Robert and Julia's parents went through an acrimonious divorce. Their father, Jim, openly blamed their mother, saying that she was "breaking up our family." He did not mention his alcoholism or recurrent gambling debts. For the most part their mother, Susan, refrained from talking about Jim. She tried to keep their communication focused on the children, not on the issues that had led to the divorce. She tried to maintain contact between the children and Jim's family, but discovered that only her soon-to-be ex-mother-in-law was open to this. Neither her father-in-law nor her two brothers-in-law wanted anything to do with Susan.

One month before Julia's ninth birthday, when Susan brought up the issue of a party, Julia said that she didn't want one. At first she would not say why. Susan let the issue drop for the moment, but mentioned it to Julia's teacher, with whom she was in regular contact with. Three days later the teacher called and informed Susan that Julia didn't want a party because she wanted to avoid the tension that now pervaded the house whenever both her parents were there together. She would have wanted to have the party at the house that she and Robert had moved into with Susan, but feared offending her father. Finally, although her extended family had always come to her birthday parties before, she was aware of the alienation that had set in and wasn't sure who would come this time or how they would act.

At age eight, Julia was already on the verge of assuming the role of a peacemaker and a conciliator. If her mother had gone along with Julia's wishes this could well have become a role that Julia embraced for the rest of her life.

Child-Centered Divorce

This brief story contains several valuable lessons for parents who are in the midst of separation and divorce. The first lesson is that children will quickly learn to edit what they say in order not to offend or alienate a parent. Both Robert and Julia were very uncomfortable, for example, when Jim would openly put down Susan, but neither ever expressed this openly. And Julia resisted telling Susan why she did not want a birthday party. As you will see when we address the issue of talking to children about divorce, parents must understand and respect this reticence. Open and honest communication will only come when children feel it is safe to do so.

A second lesson is this: The business of childhood and adolescence is growing up. Children and teens are quite capable of empathy, thoughtfulness, and generosity (as long as these qualities of character are modeled for them). At the same time, they are necessarily concerned with themselves and their own lives. Childhood and adolescence is fraught with its own challenges and crises. The nitty-gritty of their parents' divorce does not and should not be something that children be asked to digest, much less approve of or take sides on.

Third, children survive the upheaval that divorce creates in their lives to the extent that those who love them, including parents and extended family, are able to set aside issues of loyalty or feelings of resentment and focus instead on the developmental needs of the child. In the above example, that would have meant that the whole family celebrate Julia's birthday. After all, that day is about Julia, not about anyone else. If such a celebration proved impossible, then two separate celebrations might be held, but in neither case should the focus of the day be on anything except Julia.

Research has shown that if separated parents are able to minimize overt conflict between them in the presence of their children, then frequent contact with their "non-residential" parent is associated with better overall adjustment. In contrast, more frequent contact actually has an adverse effect on adjustment when visits are accompanied by a great deal of overt conflict. This is all the more reason for separated parents to cooperate as best they can so as to produce a child-focused divorce.

Staying on Track

Things go awry for the divorced child when the focus of the parents or extended family becomes the divorce itself as opposed to the developmental needs of the children. That is not to say that the divorced child should become a spoiled child; rather, it means that efforts need to be made to preserve things such as attachments that have been formed to adults, the rules and structure of daily life, and friendships that have been established. That is what I mean by a "child-centered divorce." Too often parents and families allow themselves to be led by their emotions in directions that stray from this focus. To the extent that you, the reader, can avoid this, you will also help to insure that your child comes through these three years a stronger and more resilient individual.

Chapter 2

Talking to Children about Divorce

The Explanation Trap

Lisa and Bill, who had been married for eighteen years, decided to wait until the end of the school year to tell their two teenage children that they were splitting. They did this because they did not want to disrupt their children's school work. In addition, they agreed to use the word "separation" instead of "divorce," feeling that that word was softer, and to tell the children that it was a "trial," whereas in truth their separation was final.

On the last day of school, Lisa and Bill sat their son and daughter down and broke the news. Their daughter, age twelve, immediately broke down. Then their fourteen-year-old son asked a simple question: "Why?" At that point Lisa proceeded to try to explain how she and Bill had "drifted apart" and had "different priorities and goals." And so on. In less than a minute Lisa realized that she had made a big mistake—there was no way that her two children were going to understand *why* their parents were splitting. Each of them knew plenty of other kids whose parents were divorced, and both children immediately made it known that none of these kids had anything good to say about it.

The lesson to be learned from this short story is this: Never try to explain to your children *why* you are getting a divorce. There are three reasons for this:

1. They will try to talk you out of it. Children and teens—and often even adult children—can easily turn the tables and put pressure on parents to justify their decision to separate. Or, they may come up with ideas for how you can stay together.

2. It is virtually impossible to explain your side of the story without seeking to gain support and sympathy. I have never heard a divorcing parent offer a truly objective and unbiased explanation for their decision. This then puts children in the position of having to choose which parent's justification they want to align themselves with.

3. It is important to think about how you want your children to think about the institution of marriage, as they will also likely be married one day. Do you want them to regard marriage as a fundamentally private matter between spouses, or as an open book? Personally I prefer the former.

What children *do* need to know is how their parents' separation and divorce will affect them on a day-to-day, week-to-week basis. For example:

- Will I have to move?
- Will I stay in the same school?
- Will I be rotating between my parents, and, if so, what will that look like?
- With whom will I be spending holidays?
- Will I be able to maintain contact with friends?
- Will I still see my extended family?
- What will I do in the summer? (especially important for teens)

Your goal as a separated parent is to help your child cope effectively with the crisis that your divorce represents. If you do this successfully, your child will come through this crisis not just unharmed, but potentially more resilient and able to handle whatever other crises may come along. At the same time, you need to recognize that your child may never fully understand, much less approve of, your decision. You only have to justify your decision to one person: yourself. No matter how good their intentions may be, parents like Lisa and Bill inevitably find themselves in a very uncomfortable position if they try to explain their decision to their children. So, then, what do you do?

Keep It Simple

Regardless of whether your child is eight or eighteen, the first rule to keep in mind when talking about divorce is to let your child *that* you are getting a divorce, not *why* you are getting a divorce. If you are asked why, simply say something like "*the reasons are too complicated to explain and you don't really need to know them.*" The bottom line is that the family structure your children have become accustomed to is about to change. What they do need to know is that their parents will no longer be living under the same roof, and how that change in turn will affect their own day-to-day lives.

Toddlers and younger children need to know only the most basic information, as the very concept of divorce is not something they can fully comprehend (similarly, although they may know that Mommy and Daddy are married, they may not comprehend the meaning of that term in the same way that you as an adult do).

An acceptable explanation of divorce to a young child is something like this: "*Mommy and Daddy are going to each have their own house to live in and you will be spending time in each place. So you will be having two beds, one at Mommy's and one at Daddy's.*"

If your child is a preschooler the first thing you need to do is decide where each of you will be living once you separate. If you are the parent who will be moving out, you should be prepared to take your child or children to your new place and give them a tour. Be sure to show your child the room that he or she will be sleeping in. Both parents need to decide together which prized possessions their child will be able to take along to the new house, as well as which ones he or she will be able to take back and forth. Expect young children to want to bring along a bunch of favorite stuffed animals and toys if they will be dividing their time between two households. Your child may well ask about this when you first announce your divorce, so try to be prepared in advance with an answer.

If your child is an adolescent, the explanation of the divorce can be a bit more specific, but you should still refrain from going into the reasons for your decision. You can use any term you like—divorce, separation, trial separation—but be sure to explain clearly where each parent will be living. Teens are particularly concerned about whether divorce means they will have to relocate, make new friends, or change schools. Be sure to address these issues right away. You can defer any discussion of shared parenting (how much time the teen can expect to spend at each parent's home), unless you happen to know exactly what that will be. Generally speaking, adolescents, as opposed to younger children, need to feel that they have at least some say in these arrangements, and that visitation schedules will not mean having to give up their favored activities.

What to Expect:
From Denial to Reluctant Acceptance

Parents often express fears that their child will break down and get upset when they announce their decision to divorce. They act as if they somehow believe this would be a terrible thing. Whether they realize this consciously or nor, their goal is to have their child hear this terrible news without having an emotional reaction. This, of course, is unrealistic.

There is nothing to fear from children crying upon learning that their parents are divorcing. They are being told that their life is about to be seriously disrupted, and that whatever relationships they have had with their parents are also about to change. Rather than attempting to minimize or deny those facts—or trying to do everything you can to avoid causing any upset—it is much healthier to expect this upsetting news to upset your child.

The reactions you may get can vary from the pretty bland (among toddlers and very young children) to tears and anxiety (among older children) to stony anger (among teens). You must accept these reactions and even support them. Do not, for example, attempt to talk an angry teen out of that anger. If a child cries, comfort him or her but avoid saying something "It's going to be okay, don't cry."

Here are the stages that you most often see in children and adolescents as they process a traumatic event:

- *Denial.* Children's first reaction to being told that their parents are getting a divorce is simply not to believe it. They may act as if they literally do not hear what is being said to them. They may show no reaction at all, and instead turn their attention to something else.

  One father described telling his five-year-old son that he and the boy's mother were getting a divorce. "I asked him if he knew what divorce was, and he nodded. Then he turned away and started playing with his hot wheel cars, just as he was before I told him about the divorce. He didn't miss a beat!"

  The mother of a fourteen-year-old girl reported the following reaction from her daughter: "I was positive my daughter knew that my husband and I had been having serious trouble for well over a year, but when I sat her down and told her we were getting a divorce she stood up and shouted at me, 'No, you're not!' Then she turned around and walked out of the house."

Reactions like the above do occur sometimes and they more or less fit into *denial*. In other words, when faced with a sudden, serious loss, some people initially respond by believing it just didn't happen. If your child responds this way, your best course of action is to simply give reality some time to sink in. You can expect further reactions once it does.

- *Anger*. The fourteen-year-old daughter mentioned above was actually expressing both denial and some anger when she shouted at her mother. Why anger? Because when someone takes something valuable away from us it is a natural human reaction to get angry. In this case you are taking family life as he or she knows it from your child. Your response? Accept your child's right to be angry, while making sure that anger remains within acceptable limits. When one ten-year-old boy started expressing his anger by taking scissors to his father's car seats, the father had to put a stop to it. However, he did allow his son to shout out his displeasure about the divorce as much as the boy wanted to. The father even told his son that he was sorry to have get a divorce, but that it had to happen.

- *Bargaining*. As it applies to children of divorce, the most common form of bargaining parents are apt to see will come from older children and teens. One teenage son, when told by both parents that they were getting a divorce, responded by saying, "Can't you just stay together and not talk to each other?" In other words, this teen was trying to broker a bargain between his parents that would avert the divorce and keep his lifestyle intact.

- *Sadness*. This stage you will almost certainly see. As mentioned earlier, expect there to be tears. By all means, comfort your child as best you can, but don't try to force your comfort on your child. He or she has a right to be sad. Also, just because your child isn't crying, don't assume that he or she is happy.

- *Acceptance*. This has proven to be the most controversial of the stages of grief laid out by Elisabeth Kubler-Ross. Some have argued that one never truly "accepts" a significant loss, and this may be true. At the same time, research has shown that most children seem to be capable of weathering the storm of divorce and emerging from it unscathed. That, in fact, is what this book is all about. What you can expect, then, is not necessarily for your child to express gratitude to you for divorcing so much as to survive the crisis and come out of it even stronger than before.

Don't Seek Support from Children

Parents who feel betrayed by their spouses are vulnerable to seeking out allies who will sympathize with them. This temptation can grow stronger if the divorce process becomes contentious. Seeking support, parents will sometimes share information about the divorce process with their children in an attempt to build a coalition. One father, for example, told his two teenage sons that their mother was out to force his business into bankruptcy. A distraught mother told her children that their father would not agree to pay for their college education. These issues may represent very real threats to the parents who are divorcing, but they should not be shared with children. Again, research has shown that it is not divorce itself, but intense conflict, along with attempts to lure children into taking sides, that increases the likelihood that children will emerge from the divorce deeply wounded.

Issues that children who take sides can be left to deal with three years later include guilt over aligning with one or the other parent; in other words, for abandoning the other parent. In this situation children can't win. The only possible way a child or teen can emerge from divorce as stronger individuals is to reject either parent's attempts to get them to take sides. Few children have the fortitude to do so if they are pressured by their parents to take sides.

* * *

Part Two of this book is devoted to you, the parent. The reason for including this material is to help you take care of yourself. By doing so you will be in a better position to guide your child through these three crucial years. It is recommended that you review that material periodically and conduct your own "mental health check" every so often. Remember, these times are stressful for you as well as your child. You are human, and you have your limits just as anyone else does. If you feel that you may be slipping with respect to any of the areas covered in Part One, by all means take care of yourself. By doing so you will also be taking care of your child.

Chapter 3

Relocating

Focus on the Children

Effectively coaching children through the crisis of divorce is largely a matter of monitoring their development and being alert for any negative impact that the divorce process may be having on them. An analogy would be putting an infant to sleep for the night and then checking in every so often to see that all is well. If nothing seems awry, no action is necessary. So it is with helping your children emerge from your divorce in as good (and possibly even better) psychological shape than they were before.

Children and teens are focused primarily on themselves, and rightfully so. That isn't to say that they cannot be loving or giving, because they certainly can be. Few things warm a parent's heart more than a child's gift of a drawing, an offer to share a favorite dessert, or a homemade birthday card. Nevertheless, the main business of childhood and adolescence is growing up, and as a result we should expect their focus to primarily be on the various critical developmental tasks that will be described later in the book in more detail. For toddlers, those tasks include security and exploration. For older children, these developmental tasks shift to socialization and literacy. For teens the task is identity development.

Having bought this book, you now have in your hands a road map that shows you what key developmental tasks your child is facing now and will be facing in the next three years. Armed with this knowledge, you will be in a position to understand how your divorce may potentially impact your child's ongoing development. For example, if literacy and socialization are your child's primary developmental tasks right now, you will need to be sure to monitor schoolwork, especially in the critical areas of reading and math. Should your child begin to fall behind, a simple intervention—such as taking some extra time every day to read with your child—may be all that is needed. Working in concert with your child's teacher is also very helpful, as they can steer you toward age-appropriate titles. Taking these actions will ensure that you are dealing with developmental issues head on and early on, so as to avoid problems later on.

No Surprises

One of the great myths of childhood is the idea that children are fragile. This belief motivates a surprising number of parents to try to see to it that their child (or teen) is never exposed to frustration or failure. On some level these parents believe that experiencing frustration or failure will somehow traumatize children and leave them with permanent psychological wounds.

The reality is that human beings are not fragile, physically or psychologically. If we were, we would no doubt have gone extinct a long time ago. Children and adults can be traumatized, but they are also remarkably resilient and have an amazing capacity to recover from both physical and psychological traumas. Learning to persevere in the face of frustration, to try again in the face of failure, and to adapt in the face of crisis all build what is commonly referred to as *character*.

Divorce is certainly a crisis in a child or adolescent's life. However, it does not have to leave them permanently wounded. One factor that plays a role in how well people cope with crises is the *predictability* of the crisis itself. To take an example from the adult world, consider the issue of getting laid off from a job. One thing we know is that individuals fare much better in coping with that particular crisis if they are forewarned of its possibility. That advance warning enables them to anticipate the crisis and to plan for it. They can rehearse the layoff in their mind so that, if it becomes a reality, they will at least have thought about it and had a chance to come to terms with the anxiety it provokes. They can also think about what they might do to ease the blow. Divorcing children can do the same if they are forewarned at least a few months in advance of their parents' split.

It may not really make sense for parents to inform a child that they *may* get a divorce. However, for the above reasons, it is important that divorcing parents give their children some advance warning of potential or impending changes that will result from the divorce. These include having to relocate, change schools, or give up some important aspect of a child's lifestyle, such as a special hobby or activity.

Parents should not expect a child to react with pleasure to a forewarning. However, advance warning will allow children some time to play it out in their heads, to work through some of their anxiety, and perhaps even to begin planning for how they will adapt to the change.

Reactions to Relocation

Relocating is probably the one consequence of divorce that adolescents object to the most. Younger children may not express their opposition or distress as vocally as teens are apt to do. However, having to relocate—especially if it means moving to another town and changing school districts—can disrupt even younger children's development. Your child is no doubt in the process of establishing friendships in your neighborhood and at school. You will need to do what you can to help preserve and facilitate these relationships. Children who experience a severe disruption in the socialization process—for example, by having to relocate to a different town—may become reticent to establish new friendships. It is by no means impossible for them to make new friends, but they may need to be given some structure for doing so, such as being signed up for an activity they are interested in where they will meet other children in their age group.

For teens, relocating is even more complex, for they are not only continuing the process of socialization, but are also in the midst of consolidating their identity. As described earlier, the various groups within their social sphere play a role in identity development. If they are forced to leave a group they identify with, or cannot find a comparable group they can identify with after they move, this can cause them considerable consternation.

One divorcing mother had a son who, at ten, was in the earlier stage of socialization, and a daughter who was in her second year of high school (and therefore in search of an identity). This woman and her husband attempted to make their divorce as painless as possible for their children. Thanks in part to a generous divorce settlement, she was able to purchase another house not far from the affluent town the children had so far grown up in. Still, that meant having to change schools.

This mother went to considerable pains to make the transition as easy as possible. She took the children shopping and let them pick out the décor they wanted for their new bedrooms. She offered to drive the kids to see their friends pretty much whenever they wanted. Finally, she was able to promise that they could continue their favorite out-of-school sports activities.

The above efforts met with different results. Their son had little to say regarding the divorce, and showed little in the way of an emotional reaction. He and his father had always a close relationship, and a few months after his father moved out, leaving him behind, his grades in school began to slip. His parents spoke with his teachers, who explained that their son was not turning in all his homework assignments. In addition, his teachers believed that the son might have been a little depressed about the divorce. However, like most boys, he did not particularly want to talk about it. Two of the boy's teachers suggested that maybe he should spend a little more time on school nights with his father, who had always been the one to check his homework.

Now, this mother could have reacted to what was happening with her son defensively. She could have taken the teachers' suggestion as criticism of her, or of her parenting skills. But, to her credit, she did not. Instead, she and her ex-husband agreed that their son would spend three nights each week at his father's place, and that the father would oversee the boy's homework, as he had before. They also agreed that he would accompany his son to the boy's soccer games. Four weeks later, the son was no longer missing assignments and was pulling his grades up.

As for the teenage daughter, her reaction was quite different. She hated the idea that her parents were getting a divorce, and she was very verbal about it. She directed the lion's share of her anger at her mother. She became moody and irritable, and, although she continued to maintain good grades at school, she loudly and frequently declared that she hated her new school, including the teachers, the building, and the other kids. In general she was pretty miserable to be around. As for visiting her father, she took to using schoolwork as an excuse for staying away, pretty much limiting her time with her father to dinner once during the week and an overnight every other weekend.

The difference between these children's reactions was baffling to their parents, but it becomes easily understandable once you realize the different developmental tasks these two children were dealing with. In the son's case, the basic issues for him were to maintain his relationship with his father and to be able to continue playing soccer and seeing his old friends. But for their daughter, an adolescent in search of an identity, changing schools upset her apple cart in a major way. True, she could still maintain contact with her old friends, but every day at school she felt like a stranger in a strange land. Although no one was unfriendly toward her, everyone seemed to be fairly established in one group or another. She was invited to parties, but she still felt like an outsider.

This teen's crisis was resolved by speaking to a counselor. The counselor suggested that she appeared to have carved out something of an identity among her old friends and in her old school, and that this identity was recognized and accepted there. In contrast, when she walked into the new high school it was as if she did not know who she was. The girl agreed with this assessment. That being true, the counselor suggested that this teen had some options. She could continue to build her identity around her old friends, and spend all of her free time with them. That would mean, however, not looking for a group to fit into in the new school. Alternatively, she could maintain her former affiliations and look at the new school as an opportunity to experiment, socially speaking, so as to broaden her overall social network. The daughter then determined that the latter option was not only in her best interest, but it was the most intriguing.

This teen's parents could have told their daughter the same thing that the counselor did (and so can you). The only real difference was that her parents did not address their daughter's identity issue, while the counselor recognized and addressed it.

Promote a Resilient Approach to Life

The concept of resilience will be discussed many times in this book, and it is critical to determining how parents and children alike respond to a crisis such as divorce: Whether they will come through divorce unscathed and perhaps even stronger, or whether they will come through it feeling emotionally wounded and weakened. Resilience reveals itself both in our thinking and our behavior. It is also modeled by children on their parents.

In terms of thinking, resilience involves the following beliefs:

- That occasional crises are a normal part of life and should be expected to occur now and then;

- That life—including its crises—has meaning and that we can learn from crises;
- That it is possible to come through a crisis stronger. The keys to this are perseverance and flexibility.

Parents can greatly enhance their children's ability to cope with divorce and emerge from its three crucial years emotionally stronger by modeling the above approach to life.

Chapter 4

Shared Parenting:
The New Look in
Child Custody

For many years judges who heard divorce cases that involved children made custody decisions based on the assumption that children—particularly young children, but also children as old as thirteen—needed to be primarily with their mothers in order to develop properly. This was popularly known as the *tender years doctrine*. This doctrine prevailed in American courts from the late nineteenth century until fairly recently. Today the tender years doctrine—and in turn child custody arrangements—is fast being replaced by the idea of *shared parenting*.

Shared parenting is based on a different assumption, which is usually referred to as the *best interests of the child doctrine*. This doctrine is interpreted in many courts to mean that children—including very young children—develop most healthily if they spend approximately equal amounts of time with each parent. Several state courts have even ruled that the tender years doctrine violates fathers' constitutional rights. These rulings have resulted in more movement toward shared parenting. As a result, it is not unusual today to find fathers and mothers of children as young as three or four splitting their time with a child about fifty-fifty.

Shared parenting, or what is sometimes called *co-parenting*, makes sense on one level. As cited earlier, more frequent contact with *both* parents tends to be associated with happier, healthier children. However, this tends to be true only when there is not a lot of overt conflict between the divorcing parents. Therefore, it cannot be said that shared parenting is *inevitably* better than an arrangement, say, in which one parent has primary residence and the other has a fixed visitation schedule. What may matter most in the latter instance is whether the nonresidential parent is reliable with respect to visitation. There is no sadder story to be heard than that of a child who waits for Dad (or Mom) to show up, only to get stood up.

Time in the Trenches: Assessing Parenting Experience

As appealing as the idea of shared parenting may be, there may be as many potential hazards in it as there were in the tender years doctrine. In other words, neither doctrine may hold true all the time. Unfortunately, the law is often referred to as a crude instrument, not given to making fine distinctions. Therefore, once a doctrine becomes established it tends to be applied as a rule with few exceptions.

If you and your former spouse are debating (or contesting!) the issue of shared parenting, one factor that should play a role in whatever living arrangements are *initially* made for your child is just how much of the day-to-day, week-to-week, "grunt work" of parenting each of you has done up until this point. The following questionnaire can be useful for this.

Taken together, these questions can be taken as a measure of just how much you "walk the walk" of parenting. These tasks constitute the grunt work referred to above. The more of this hands-on parenting you personally do, the more ready you are for true, fifty-fifty co-parenting. Conversely, the less of the grunt work you have done so far, the less prepared you are for co-parenting right now. That isn't to say that you will never be ready for full co-parenting; just that you are not there at this point. Therefore, you need a plan that can guide you in that direction.

Parents who are less experienced in the kind of hands-on parenting described in the above questionnaire may be able to learn "on the job," as they say. However, while they are doing this, their children are put in the awkward position of having to educate their parents in the day-to-day, week-to-week responsibilities of their own parenting. Children may also feel somewhat anxious during this stage, since the support they have come to rely on from the parent who formerly had done the lion's

Shared Parenting Inventory

Instructions: Answer each of the following questions as it applies to you now.

- Do you know the name of your child's pediatrician?
- How often have you brought your child to a pediatrician appointment?
- Do you know the name and phone number of your child's school nurse?
- Do you know the name and phone number (or e-mail address) of your child's teacher?
- Does your child take any medications? If so, do you know their names, doses, and when your child is supposed to take them?
- Do you know approximately your child's weight and height today?
- How many days in the past two years have you taken off from work in order to stay home with your child when she or he was sick?
- If your child is in day care, how often in the past year have you had a one-to-one chat with the director of the day care center about your child's progress in socialization?
- How often do you supervise or help your child with his or her homework?
- What are your child's favorite television shows?
- How often do you read to your child?
- How many days per week do you supervise your child while he or she gets ready for bed, including brushing teeth, washing up, and getting into pajamas?
- How often do you prepare a meal for your child?
- What are your child's favorite foods, and which are his or her least favorites?
- How often do you purchase clothing for your child? Do you know what his or her current clothing sizes are?
- Do you know the names of your child's best friends?
- How many of your child's birthday parties have you personally organized and supervised?

share of parenting may be unavailable while they are with the less experienced parent.

Walking the Walk: Matching Co-Parenting to Parenting Experience

My personal bias is to try to roughly match initial visiting and custody arrangements with each parent's level of parenting experience. For example, if reality shows that one parent has had 75 percent of the parenting experience described in the questionnaire, while the other has had only 25 percent, after the divorce children should divide their time between the parents in roughly the same proportions, at least initially.

Over time the less experienced parent should be given opportunities to "catch up" in the day-to-day parenting; for example, by taking the child or children to pediatrician appointments, by cooking family meals, and by supervising bedtime preparation. Then, as the less experienced parent begins to catch up, living schedules can gradually move toward a true fifty-fifty split. This gradual increase avoids making the child or children anxious and avoids having to separate a great deal from the parent who early had done most of the parenting.

Some people who read this may object to this recommendation. They may feel that they have parental rights that entitle them to "equal ownership" of their child or children, regardless of how much actual nuts-and-bolts parenting experience they may have. Indeed, these parents may find that a court is sympathetic to this view. However, I would maintain that this legal bias should not be confused with what is truly in the best interests of their child's or children's development. Children are much more likely to emerge from the divorce three years later in better psychological shape if their parents first took stock of their actual parenting experience. If, in doing so, they realize that there is a significant imbalance, they should devise a schedule for their children that allows the less experienced parent some time to build up what might be called their "parental resume" over time. Two examples illustrate this.

Martin and Mary

At the time they decided to divorce, Martin and Mary had one child, a six-year-old son named Jason. Martin, who was outraged over Mary's decision to leave him, came to believe that she was also trying to exclude him from his son's life. He reacted by hiring an attorney who was well known for his litigious style, and pressed his case for full shared parenting. His lawyer proposed a complex schedule for Jason to divide his time, a month at a time, exactly fifty-fifty between Martin and Mary. This schedule was so complicated that Jason would have to keep a copy of it in his school backpack, where he could refer to it every day. In addition, because it involved Jason taking a different school bus to and from school on different days on different weeks, both his parents and the school would also have to keep Jason's schedule posted somewhere.

Mary objected to this plan. She pointed out to the attorney who was assigned the task of representing Jason's best interests that at that point Martin did not even have a child safety seat in his car. Martin, she insisted, never took Jason anywhere, and never in his car. Martin did not know the name of Jason's pediatrician, or the names of any of the staff in the day care center he attended Monday through Friday. Indeed, as measured by the parenting inventory, Martin thus far had spent very little time "in the trenches," doing the day-to-day tasks of parenting his son.

In this case, jumping immediately into a fifty-fifty co-parenting arrangement would not seem to be in the best interests of Jason. Instead, it seems obvious that Jason's continued healthy development would be better served by some arrangement that allowed Martin to build his parenting abilities. This might involve some coaching by a family therapist, with the arrangement monitored by Jason's attorney.

Philip and Jessica

Philip and Jessica had started dating in their sophomore year of college. Theirs was a somewhat tumultuous relationship marked by several break-ups and reconciliations. Four years later they got engaged. Philip had a good job in the information technology field, and Jessica had landed an entry-level job in financial services. Then she got pregnant.

About two months before their scheduled wedding and with Jessica eight months pregnant, she called it off. Her reason was the ongoing backbiting and squabbling that hung like a cloud over their relationship. She had concluded that it would never end.

Up until the time that Jessica called off the wedding, Philip had been going with her to virtually every one of her obstetrician's appointments.

The two had also attended childbirth classes together. However, in her anger Jessica wanted as little to do with Philip as possible. She let it be known that her intention was to raise their child by herself, with no involvement on his part. When she went into labor she did not tell Philip, and he was replaced in the hospital birthing room by Jessica's mother.

Philip was quite depressed about Jessica's decision to cancel the wedding, and more than a little disconcerted over being excluded from the birth of their son. He sensed that this time there would be no reconciliation between him and Jessica. At the same time, he very much wanted to be part of his child's life.

In this instance, the court also assigned the child an attorney to represent its best interests. Working with that attorney, as well as with a counselor, and using the leverage of the court, Philip stated that he wanted to be a father to his son. He voiced no reservations about participating in every parenting task, from changing diapers, to feeding, to taking his son to pediatrician appointments. Despite Jessica's ongoing objections, by the time the boy was two years old he was being co-parented just about equally by his two parents.

* * *

The difference between the above two examples is that in one instance a father simply wanted to assert his right to co-parent as if his child were a piece of property. In contrast, in the second instance a father truly was willing to do whatever it took to parent his child.

I am not an attorney; much less a judge. The current proclivity of courts to decide child-custody arrangements with an eye toward co-parenting will probably continue. Therefore, if you are a divorcing parent I can only urge you to take the material presented here into account. Remember that change itself is not so threatening to your child's psychological welfare as chaos and unpredictability. Thrusting a child into a situation with a parent who has had relatively little hands-on experience may very well not be in that child's long-term best interest.

Chapter 5

New Beginnings

Even as the divorce of its parents marks the end of a chapter in a child's life, for most a new chapter will begin at some point in the three crucial years that are the subject of this book. That new chapter will begin when the child is introduced to a parent's new "friend" and will continue if a new relationship is established and a new family begins to emerge.

Introducing New Partners to Children

If you are someone who is not basically a loner, but rather enjoys being in a relationship, chances are that sooner or later you will begin to look around for a potential partner. You may want to remarry; alternatively, you may conclude that having a commitment is enough, without the need to marry. In either case you will eventually be faced with the issue of disclosing this relationship to your child, and of introducing your child to your new partner or prospective partner.

There are two basic rules to keep in mind when doing this:

- *No surprises*
  Once again remembering that change per se is not as stressful as is unpredictability, it is vital that divorced or divorcing parents not "spring" a new partner on their children. Children and teens can cope very well with change; indeed, they and their world are in a more or less continual state of change as they grow. At the same time they rely on a certain amount of stability and predictability to balance that change. Woe be to the parent who brings home their new boyfriend or girlfriend unannounced!

As much as this rule might sound like common sense, it really is surprising just how many divorcing parents violate it. One father, for example, told his twelve-year-old daughter that they were going to Boston for the day to visit a couple of museums. What he left out was that they would be driving there and spending the day with his new "friend" and her ten-year-old son. Not wishing to displease her father the girl went along, but was obviously miserable the whole time. Afterward the father questioned her, going so far as to suggest she had been rude. At that point the girl totally lost her composure, broke down in tears, and yelled at her father, "You need to tell me first if you want me to meet a girlfriend!" When this father later told his girlfriend about this interaction— and the girlfriend realized that that he had failed to tell his daughter ahead of time that the two would be meeting—the girlfriend also let the father have it! Obviously, this was not the way to get this new relationship off on the right foot.

- *Easy does it*
  This is a corollary to the first rule. As much as divorcing parents may want their children to meet someone who they think is the greatest thing that's ever happened to them, children and teens need to have some control over just how fast this process moves. One important factor that plays a role here is the issue of *loyalty*. Here is an example of how this works.

Carl and Martha had one of those unfortunately contentious divorces in which one parent in particular attempted to enlist the sympathy and support of their two children, Emily, who was a freshman in high school, and Harry, who was in sixth grade. While Harry dealt with the divorce by more or less keeping his distance and spending a lot of time in his room playing his guitar and playing video games, Emily apparently felt some obligation to spend time with her mother, listening to her many complaints about Carl. For his part, Carl pretty much avoided talking to his children about Martha and the divorce. On the few occasions that Emily brought it up, hinting at asking why it had happened, Carl cut the conversation short. He did not feel it was useful for the kids to know what went wrong with their parents' marriage.

According to Harry and Emily, Martha did not go into detail about her marital problems either. However, Martha did complain—often and bitterly—that Carl was trying to make her suffer, for example, by being ungenerous with child support. She also made comments now and then that Carl was selfish and more concerned with his personal comfort than with taking care of his family.

These unfortunate family dynamics, which are all too common during divorces, created a situation that was very uncomfortable for the children. Emily confided to a therapist she was seeing that she did not like listening to her mother's complaints or her criticisms about her father, yet she felt some obligation to support her mother. Harry, who continued to avoid things as much as possible, nevertheless felt some of this same obligation, for whenever his mother did catch him in a situation that he could not escape—for example, talking him shopping for a new pair of athletic shoes—he did not speak up in his father's defense.

This is a situation of *coerced loyalty*, meaning that neither Emily nor Harry were free to pursue their relationships with both their parents in an unfettered manner. Rather, they felt compelled to support their mother and sympathize with her more so than their father. This issue became evident in two ways. First, Emily resisted spending as much time with Carl as he would have liked and was entitled to under the terms of the divorce decree. She made excuses such as having made commitments to spend time with friends, and that she did not like the longer school bus ride she had to take if she stayed overnight at Carl's place.

Second, Emily began making negative comments when she suspected that her father was dating, which in fact he was. These comments struck Carl as echoes of what Emily might be hearing at home. For example, during one phone conversation Emily said, out of the blue, "When you find a girlfriend I hope she's not a lot younger than you are." Another time, when Carl, Emily, and Harry were out having a pizza together, Emily said, "My best friend Eliza's father has a new girlfriend that Eliza just can't stand."

An attitude such as the one that Emily was voicing clearly complicates the issue of starting over and introducing a new partner into a child's life. In this case it was the loyalty that Emily felt obliged to give to her mother that was standing in the way of her being open to meeting her father's new friend. For her part Martha may have felt she had her children's loyalty, but in truth this loyalty was not freely given. Worse, it was likely to leave both of her children to deal with the guilt, at some point down the road, of having betrayed their father.

If you find yourself caught in this sort of situation the best course of action is to follow an old maxim often voiced among recovering alcoholics: *Easy does it!* As much as it may frustrate you to have to put off introducing someone you've met and like a great deal to your child, you are better off putting that on hold for a while. Imagine how it would have complicated this scenario had Carl tried to introduce a new girlfriend to Emily and Carl too quickly.

Experience teaches us that coerced loyalty can only go so far and last so long. As time passes, and if you follow the guidelines offered in this book, you will find that your bond with your child grows stronger and stronger. At some point your child will give you a sign that she or he is no longer willing to sacrifice his or her relationship with you just to maintain a coerced loyalty to your ex-spouse. That will be the time to move ahead and bring your child into your newly developing relationship.

Blended Families: First Steps

Many divorced men and women say that being a stepparent is the most difficult and uncomfortable role they can imagine. They also say that they had no idea ahead of time just what it would be like. The subject of stepparenting can be (and has been) the subject of an entire separate book. As far as this book is concerned you need to have a few guidelines as to how to *begin* this process of forming a new, so-called blended family.

Meet-and-Greet

You could say that a blended family begins as soon as you, your child or children, your new partner, and his or her child or children meet for the first time. There's a saying goes: *You only have one chance to make a first impression.* Therefore, this first meeting can be important. For the same reason it can also be stressful and uncomfortable for all involved.

One way to reduce the stress of introducing someone new in your life to your child is to have an agenda for this initial meeting that will help to make it pleasant and which can be used as a focus for the event. Ideas for doing this include doing something together as a group, such as going to a sporting event or museum, or centering it on a holiday such as the Fourth of July. One set of parents decided to introduce their four children to each other by having a Fourth of July barbecue and then going to a fireworks show afterward. Another used a child's birthday as a reason to host a pool party. Some of the birthday child's friends and parents also attended, which helped to keep the atmosphere light.

A second ground rule for these initial meetings is to keep them time limited. In the examples just given, the Fourth of July barbecue was held in the early evening and lasted a few hours. The two parents then took separate cars to the fireworks show, said goodbye when it ended, and took their respective children home. The invitation to the birthday party specified that it would run from noon to 3 p.m. on a Saturday. The visiting new boyfriend made sure he left with his child when all the other children were picked up.

Structuring the first two or three meetings between two families that potentially will become one can go a long way toward reducing stress. You cannot, of course, force a child to be happy about the prospect of moving into a blended family. Children naturally have anxieties about this. This is even more true if the new family will include any children approximately their age. As human beings we are instinctively social creatures; part of our instinct has to do with where we fit into a social hierarchy, and families are social hierarchies. So if there is a possibility that your child may potentially be part of a blended family you can expect you child to wonder just where she or he will fit in on the social totem pole.

In the case described earlier, Carl would have to expect Emily to have a negative attitude toward any woman he might want her to meet. As things stood Emily really was not free to like any woman—no matter how likable she might be—because to do so would be to betray her loyalty to her mother. In such cases it is best not to force the issue. Carl was free to date, of course. He did not, however, need to press his daughter to meet any of these women. If and when he believed he found a woman who he wanted to make a commitment to, his best course of action would be to share this with his son and daughter, and then to arrange two or three "meet-and-greet" occasions such as those described above. However, he would be wise to *invite* Emily and Harry to these events, but not to pressure them to attend. Eventually, the kind of coerced loyalty that Emily and Harry were bound by will usually fade, as a child wants to make his or her own decisions and maintain a relationship with both parents.

Maintaining Personal Space

Regardless of whether your child has his or her own bedroom or shares one, he or she still has a space somewhere in your home that he or she regards as personal and private. Siblings who share a room can attest to how they will divide up the space and personalize their own space, decorating it to their own taste and keeping out of each other's space.

A child who has its own room will have that much more of a sense of personal space. This issue and the concerns it can generate should not be taken for granted. Rather, it needs to be put on the table for discussion as soon as it looks like there is a good chance that two families will in fact be blending under a single roof. Expect this issue to be equally thorny regardless of who will be leaving a home—your child, or your partner's child.

You will find this issue somewhat easier to deal with if the children involved are given some advance warning that they will be living together, if there will be enough room so that they will be able to have their own room, and if they have an opportunity to arrange their new space to suit themselves. One woman, for example, showed her two young sons the new bedrooms they would each be moving into. In this case her new partner had a daughter who spent about half her time with him, and also had a room of her own. Together she and her partner took the boys to a home store where they picked out paint colors for their rooms, then to a linens store where they chose curtains and bedding. Together they painted the rooms, put up shelves, and moved furniture around until they boys felt comfortable. The result was a remarkable absence of significant tension throughout the moving-in process.

Another pair of partners came up with a particularly creative approach to dealing with the personal space issue. She, an architect, made copies of the blueprints of her home, which her fiancé and his ten-year-old son would be moving into. She gave these to her fiancé, who showed them to his son. He pointed out the bedroom the boy would be occupying, and the family room that would be the center of family activities. They used a pencil to draw different possible configurations of furniture, as well as talking about where in the family room would be the best place to put the boy's computer table and computer. When the boy visited the house, he brought his marked-up blueprints with him, and the experience turned out to be a positive one.

Making Friends, Establishing Lines of Authority

These two topics, which might strike you as contradictory, actually go hand in hand. They are reciprocal processes—two sides of one coin that represents the challenges of being a step-parent. Like personal space, this is a subject that needs to be out in the open, particularly between partners who are contemplating merging two families into one. The dialogue that needs to take place concerns any differences you may believe exist between the two of you in terms of how you discipline and reward your children, as well as the limits each of you sets. The goal is for both of you to feel that you have some authority, and for your children to respect that authority. Step-parents often feel that they lack authority, and children sometimes resent and resist it.

It can be a challenge indeed for divorced parents who are building a blended family to come to a consensus on issues such as rewards, discipline, and limits. This may well involve some compromise on both your parts. It will almost certainly involve some ongoing communication. One common—and problematic—pattern that can emerge in blended families is for each parent to feel that they are each solely responsible for supervising, rewarding, and disciplining their own children. Children and teens can easily take advantage of such as arrangement, for example by ignoring any limit imposed by their step-parent, or else seeking to have the step-parent's decisions overruled by their biological parent. This inevitably leads to a situation where each step-parent ends up bringing issues and complaints about the other's child or children to the other's attention. Meanwhile they abdicate their own responsibility for dealing with these things. Needless to say this can lead to intense stress in the relationship.

As you believe you are working toward a consensus about limits, rewards, and discipline, it is vital that you support one another in dealing directly with *all* your children in these areas. Of course you probably want to start off in small areas if that is possible, for example in reinforcing limits you have reached a consensus on.

The best parents are perceived by their children as benign authorities. That is, they are adults who set and enforce limits, provide security and affection, and dole out rewards and punishments in a fair way. They do this not because they enjoy the power of authority, but because they care about the welfare of their children. This in turn sets the stage for respect as well as friendship between parent and child. And so it is for step-parents and step-children. Strive to be this kind of benign authority in both your children's lives and the lives of any step-children you may have, and you will surely reap these rewards.

Part Two

Understanding Yourself: How to Be Part of the Solution and not Part of the Problem

This second part of the book will help you understand how, in addition to your child's or children's emotional health, your attitude toward divorce, and your attitude toward life crises in general can have a strong influence on how children emerge from the three crucial years. To sum it up, the better off you are—psychologically and spiritually—the better off your child will be.

Chapter 6

How "Resilient" Are You?

Over the past twenty years, psychologists have learned a great deal about people who are able to weather life crises and emerge pretty much unscathed, and about those who aren't. That is, not everyone is affected equally by trauma. Whereas some people survive a crisis with obvious and deep psychological wounds, others seem to be more capable of bending without breaking. They are more *resilient,* in contrast to those whose personalities could be described as *fragile.*

It turns out that there are specific and identifiable differences between resilient and fragile men and women. These differences became strikingly evident when psychologists conducted a series of studies of corporate executives. These are men and women who hold chronically stressful jobs. Problems inevitably end up on their desks, and they often have to make decisions that affect not only themselves but the welfare of many of those below them on the organization chart.

As you might expect, one group coped with the chronic stress better than others. The ones that did poorly—the psychologically fragile group—reported much higher levels of anxiety, were prone to depression, and had more problems with their physical health; for example, hypertension. This group stood in sharp contrast to the executives whose lives were just as stressful, but who did not suffer these problems.

The results of in-depth interviews and tests led to the discovery that these groups differed profoundly in terms of their outlooks on life in general, and on their jobs in particular. Specifically, the healthier, more resilient group was characterized by the following beliefs:

- *Life has meaning.*
  When they first read the above statement, some people respond by saying "That's a spiritual belief." Perhaps they are right, in the

sense that spiritual people typically do believe that life has meaning. Spiritual people believe that they are here for some purpose, and that there is something to be learned both from setbacks and successes. That's not to say that spirituality is exclusive to any particular religion. In fact, virtually all religions are based on the premise that life has meaning.

As it pertains to life crises—including divorce—this belief is consistent with psychological resilience because it encourages people to believe that the crisis itself has meaning for them, if only they are open to finding that meaning. In contrast, psychologically fragile persons are inclined to seek no meaning in crisis. They are much more likely to view themselves as victims of bad luck or, worse, of others' intentional efforts to make them miserable.

- *Crises are a normal part of life and we should expect them to occur.*
Some people believe that life is a smooth road. They are shocked to encounter a wall or an impasse or an unexpected ditch. How do you react to someone like that? Personally I want to shake them and shout, *"Wake up! This is life, not a fairy tale!"* These people are apt to react to problems as if they were more significant than they really are—and to draw from them conclusions about their own fitness, abilities, and essential characteristics. They are more likely to throw up their hands and lose control. They need to work on their resilience.

Resilient people, on the other hand, look at life with fewer expectations. They allow that there might be bumps in the road of life, and they are not overly put off when they hit one: They more or less keep their hands on the steering wheel.

- *Crises create opportunities.*
The ability to see life as both a mix of good and bad attributes is critical to the most successful corporate executives. When they encounter a crisis (e.g., a financial crisis caused by a recession), the resilient executive's first thought is not, *"Oh my God! What's going to happen to me?"* Rather, it is, *"How can I take advantage of this crisis? What do I need to do to ensure my own and my company's survival? Are there even ways that this crisis can benefit me and my company?"* So, too, can it be with divorce. The resilient parent facing divorce may very well recognize the downside of this

event, but will also look for the proverbial silver lining. Resilient people live by the motto: *Never Miss the Opportunities that Crisis Creates*. In this case, though, it is your family, not your employer, whom you want to usher through the crisis, and possibly even benefit from it.

- *We create our own luck.*

This is the opposite of believing that what happens to us in life is either the result of luck—good or bad—or of forces that are beyond our control. That is what psychologically fragile people are inclined to believe. The resilient person, though, will never accept the idea that adversity, such as poverty or illness, is sufficient reason to account for why a person does not achieve his or her potential. Resilient people are inclined to believe that overcoming adversity builds character and makes a person all the stronger for it. So it can be for divorce, for you as well as your child.

- *I can survive.*

While less resilient people harbor inner doubts about whether they can survive a crisis, resilient men and women never really doubt their ability to survive. Applied to the crisis that divorce presents us with, the resilient parent will be strong in his or her conviction that everyone will not only survive, but become stronger for it. The resilient parent believes that divorce is not a reason that children cannot achieve their potential or be happy.

The Resilience Inventory:
How Resilient Are You?

If you think about your friends or acquaintances, chances are you will be able to think of people who strike you as resilient. You may also think of some who are psychologically fragile. Most people are not either extremely resilient or fragile; instead, their personality falls somewhere between these two extremes.

To get a sense of just how resilient you are, take a few minutes to complete the following inventory. After you answer each question, total your score to come up with a personal *Resilience Index*.

Resilience Inventory

Instructions: Respond to each of the following statements in terms of how well do they describe *your personal beliefs,* from 0 (*not at all*) to 10 (*completely*). When you are finished, total your scores.

1. I believe that I was put here for a purpose: 0 1 2 3 4 5 6 7 8 9 10
2. I believe in the saying: *"For every door that closes, another door opens."* 0 1 2 3 4 5 6 7 8 9 10
3. Between the work I do and other activities, I feel that my life has meaning: 0 1 2 3 4 5 6 7 8 9 10
4. I believe it's true that every cloud has a silver lining: 0 1 2 3 4 5 6 7 8 9 10
5. No matter how bad things get, I believe I can survive a crisis: 0 1 2 3 4 5 6 7 8 9 10
6. I believe in enjoying life when all is going well, because life will inevitably throw you a curveball: 0 1 2 3 4 5 6 7 8 9 10
7. I believe that a crisis like divorce can actually make me and my child stronger and happier in the long run: 0 1 2 3 4 5 6 7 8 9 10
8. I believe that I am the master of my own fate: 0 1 2 3 4 5 6 7 8 9 10
9. It may take a while but I believe that life will be better for me and my child once my divorce is over and we can get a fresh start on life: 0 1 2 3 4 5 6 7 8 9 10
10. Happiness and success is a matter of hard work and perseverance, not luck: 0 1 2 3 4 5 6 7 8 9 10

Total Score: _____ = Your *Resilience Index*

Take a look at your Resilience Index. How accurately do you think it describes you in terms of your true beliefs? Do you think you may have slanted your answers in one direction or another? Most people, if they take some time to reflect and answer the above questions honestly, find that their Resilience Index fall somewhere in the middle range, between 25 and 75. There are, of course, exceptions: for example, people who are truly very resilient. Conversely, there are people who fall at the opposite (low) extreme. These are people who will have the hardest time getting through a crisis like divorce.

If your resilience index is above 65, consider yourself in pretty good shape to weather a crisis like divorce, and in turn to help your child weather the storm that lies ahead. Your personal health in this regard will be an asset not only to you, but to your child or children. Through your own attitudes toward life, and toward the bumps in the road that we all will inevitably confront, you will be providing your child with a model for approaching adversity. It's likely that you will see resilience build in your child as well as time goes on.

What should you do, on the other hand, if you discover that your Resilience Index falls somewhere below 65? What if it is less than 50? Does this mean that you are in for hard times? Well, the answer depends on whether you want to do something about it or not. If you feel helpless to change your outlook on life, then the next three years may indeed be painful for you as well as your children. On the other hand, if you choose to do so, it is possible to work on changing the way you approach life in general, and this divorce in particular, so as to become more resilient. The following are some guidelines for doing this.

Becoming Resilient

Here are two tried and true methods that psychologists have used to help people learn how to recover from situations.

Self-talk

Self-talk is self-affirmation, or the habit of telling yourself resilient statements such as the ones that appear in the resilience inventory. There are many ways that you can prompt yourself to challenge your self-defeatist thinking. You can begin by purchasing a weekly calendar. At the top of each week, write one encouraging statement to yourself. Each day, when you open the calendar, read that week's resilient statement to yourself. Or, write out all ten resilient beliefs and then tape them up, either at work or at home. Begin each day by reading one of the statements and taking a minute to let the idea sink in.

It may strike you as hard to believe, but self-talk has actually been found to be an effective method for changing thought patterns. The secret lies in the fact that most people are not *consciously* aware of their inner beliefs and how these beliefs affect them. Even resilient people more or less just act in resilient ways, without being aware of the underlying belief that motivates their behavior. Similarly, the nonresilient person may not be consciously aware that a tendency, for example, to get easily discouraged, is actually based on an inner belief that perseverance in the face of adversity is useless. The resilient person, in contrast, inwardly believes that perseverance usually pays off. So, if you use the self-talk technique conscientiously for a period of time, you can expect your behavior to change.

Cognitive Role Playing

The second effective method for changing beliefs (and therefore changing behavior) is called "cognitive role playing." This is just a fancy term for imagining yourself in different situations and then imagining how you would react in each situation *depending on what beliefs you held*. Here is an example of a situation that commonly comes up in the process of a divorce:

> You have been negotiating with your spouse over the issue of how much time your two children, ages six and four, will spend with each of you. You have been willing to accommodate your spouse's desire to have the kids as often as two nights a week and every other weekend. Now your attorney has left you a message that your spouse has filed a motion to have the children spend equal time with each parent, which involves a complicated schedule of movement between your two residences. You strongly suspect that your spouse's motivation is that, if this arrangement is approved, he will either not have to pay child support at all, or will pay a much reduced amount. Your concern, though, is not just the money (which you do need), but the welfare of your kids, for whom you have been the primary caretaker to this point in their lives.

There are several ways to respond to the hypothetical situation. Your response, of course, depends on what you believe about life and managing crises. Imagine being in the above situation and see how you would react if you held the following *nonresilient beliefs:*

- I'm not a fighter: there is no way I can win this fight.
- I'm at the mercy of the lawyers in this situation.
- I thought this divorce was going to be amicable.

How do you feel? If you imagine having these beliefs in this kind of situation, chances are you feel scared and powerless, and perhaps even hopeless. You may experience an urge to run and hide somewhere. You may feel you have no hope but to throw yourself at the mercy of the courts.

Now, imagine being in this same situation but try adopting these responses:

- I can work out something that will be better than this proposal, even if I have to compromise.
- Whatever happens, I will be there to make sure my children are okay, and we will come out of this just fine.
- I will be a stronger person for having fought for what I believe on this issue.

How do you feel when you view this situation through the lens of the above resilient beliefs? Do you still feel as anxious? Does the situation still seem hopeless? Do you feel like running away, or do you feel like standing your ground?

* * *

Here is another situation. This time, try imagining yourself being in this situation with the following beliefs:

- Every crisis presents opportunities.
- There is always something to learn from adversity.
- Whatever happens, I can get through this and will be okay.
- Everything happens for a reason.

Now, here is the situation:

You have been unhappy in your job for the past several years. However, you have felt obligated to stick with it if for no other

reason than it has been a reliable source of income. You have
thought about pursuing different careers, perhaps returning to
school, but like many people you have stayed where you are out
of sheer inertia. Yesterday afternoon, however, you and quite
a few others were notified that you were being laid off. You
knew that your firm was going through difficult financial times
because of foreign competition. Still, you didn't quite expect
this. At your "exit interview" you were informed that because of
your seniority you will be getting a significant severance pack-
age, after which you will be eligible for unemployment benefits
if you still have not found work.

How would it feel to be in this situation if you believed that
everything—including being laid off—happens for a purpose, and that
every crisis we face also provides us with opportunities? That would be
a resilient way to approach this crisis. Two resilient individuals I knew
who found themselves in this very position ended up, at middle age,
finding new careers to pursue. They took advantage of special student
loans that were available to pursue careers in nursing and small-business
administration, respectively. In the long run, they felt that not only were
they happier, but that there was a nice spillover to their family lives, as
they reported not only being happier when they were at home but more
able to interact with family members because they were less preoccupied
with their own unhappiness and anxieties.

You Too Can Be Resilient

Believing that you cannot change nonresilient attitudes, as well as
doubting the power of resilient attitudes toward life, are aspects of being
psychologically fragile. Becoming more resilient, in turn, begins with
facing and challenging your own pessimism. If you put some genuine
effort into following the above exercises, you *can* become a more resilient individual. This will benefit not only you, but your children, as you
navigate the difficult times and challenges that divorce represents.

Chapter 7

Your Emotional Health and Your Child

Depression and anxiety are commonplace among men and women who are going through a divorce. Anxiety or depression need not be cause for alarm *unless* it reaches the point at which it begins to compromise a parent's ability to function effectively. Unfortunately, most divorcing parents are not in a position to accurately assess their own level of anxiety and depression—and to determine if they need support—because they lack the tools to do so. As parents you spend so much time taking care of your children that it's hard to fathom that you might need someone to care of you. To further complicate matters, friends and family are typically reluctant to confront a divorcing parent, even one who seems to be seriously debilitated, for various reasons. One might be fear of rejection. Another might be the concern that the divorcing parent has too much on their plate already.

However, it is important for you to assess how much anxiety or depression may be affecting you. If you are in the beginning of the divorce process, it would be a good idea to take the questionnaires that follow. You might also retake the quiz periodically every six months. Think of it as a way of keeping tabs on your *emotional* health, just like taking your blood pressure or testing your cholesterol level periodically are ways of monitoring your *physical* health.

The idea of checking yourself out for depression and anxiety may make you uncomfortable. Some people like to believe that what they don't know can't hurt them. These people are also more likely than most to avoid routine physicals. The reality, of course, is that what you don't know definitely *can* hurt you. As is true for physical disease, early detection of your mental health makes for a much better prognosis. If you are experiencing significant symptoms of anxiety or depression, you are much better off dealing with it earlier rather than later. We'll look at the alternatives after you take some time to check out your emotional health.

Taking stock of your emotional health—and acting to improve it if necessary—is very important to your children. Whether they come through these three crucial years intact and ready to move on with their lives, or come through them with significant emotional, academic, or social problems, can hinge on your being able to maintain your own emotional balance. If your ability to function as a parent is impaired by depression or anxiety, you will not be at your best. You may not pick up on important signs that you otherwise would, and you might miss opportunities to intervene in order to keep your child on a healthy developmental track. Many adults who seek treatment for debilitating depression or anxiety can attest that as children they were affected by their own parents' problems in one or both of these areas.

The exercises that follow will help you take stock of your emotional health.

Taking Stock: *Anxiety*

To assess the extent to which anxiety may be an issue you need to address, respond to each of the following statements as they describe you *today* from 0 (*not at all*) to 10 (*completely*). When you are done, total up your score:

Anxiety Inventory

1. I am forgetful and have difficulty concentrating: 0 1 2 3 4 5 6 7 8 9 10
2. I wake up often in the midd le of the night: 0 1 2 3 4 5 6 7 8 9 10
3. I have a lot of aches and pains: 0 1 2 3 4 5 6 7 8 9 10
4. I worry a lot: 0 1 2 3 4 5 6 7 8 9 10
5. I am unable to relax: 0 1 2 3 4 5 6 7 8 9 10
6. I have difficulty breathing: 0 1 2 3 4 5 6 7 8 9 10
7. I often have indigestion: 0 1 2 3 4 5 6 7 8 9 10
8. I fear that the worst will happen: 0 1 2 3 4 5 6 7 8 9 10
9. I get easily rattled: 0 1 2 3 4 5 6 7 8 9 10
10. Sometimes my heart beats so fast that I think I might be having a heart attack: 0 1 2 3 4 5 6 7 8 9 10

Total Score: _____ = Your *Anxiety Index*

Interpreting Your Anxiety Index

Rest assured that very few people, if they answer the above questions honestly, will find that they have an anxiety index of 0. In fact, scores of less than 20 are pretty rare. However, if your anxiety index is 50 or higher, this could be a sign that you should pay attention to and address your anxiety.

Taking Stock: *Depression*

To assess the extent to which depression may be an issue you need to address, respond to each of the following statements as they describe you *today* from 0 (*not at all*) to 10 (*completely*). When you are done, total up your score:

Depression Inventory

1. I have very little energy: 0 1 2 3 4 5 6 7 8 9 10
2. I have lost interest in things I once liked to do: 0 1 2 3 4 5 6 7 8 9 10
3. I feel sad much of the time: 0 1 2 3 4 5 6 7 8 9 10
4. I cry easily: 0 1 2 3 4 5 6 7 8 9 10
5. I have a hard time falling asleep: 0 1 2 3 4 5 6 7 8 9 10
6. I have no appetite and am losing weight: 0 1 2 3 4 5 6 7 8 9 10
7. I feel like a failure: 0 1 2 3 4 5 6 7 8 9 10
8. I feel pessimistic about the future: 0 1 2 3 4 5 6 7 8 9 10
9. I find a lot of faults in myself: 0 1 2 3 4 5 6 7 8 9 10
10. I have thoughts about suicide: 0 1 2 3 4 5 6 7 8 9 10

Total Score: _____ = Your *Depression Index*

Depression, much like anxiety, is not an all-or-none kind of thing. Most if not all people will experience some degree of depression several times in their lives. Low levels of depression (depression index scores of 25 or less) most often represent reactions to an unpleasant event in a person's life. This puts their spirits low for a time. However, to the extent that a person leads a balanced lifestyle (see next exercise), he or she should bounce back from depression with little or no outside help.

A depression index of 50 or higher should send up a red flag for you. An index this high usually will be reflected in some impairment in your life. For example, you may be less effective at work, due to lowered energy levels, or because you are getting easily distracted. Your contact with friends may be drifting off. You may be spending less time doing things you once enjoyed. You feel down most of the time, and you do not feel good about yourself. From where you stand right now the future may seem bleak. As much as you may want to deny it, the depression that is weighing on you now will affect your ability to parent your child as effectively as you otherwise could.

What Do I Do Now?

Okay, so your score on one or both of the above inventories is above 50 and that worries you a bit. You are concerned for yourself, but even more you are concerned for your children. You want them to get through this divorce without any permanent scars. That means helping them process the next three crucial years. In order to do that, you know that you can't afford to be weighed down by anxiety or depression. The logical question you now need an answer to is: What can I do to fix this?

These days the most common way that men and women try to deal with anxiety or depression is through medication. We know this because they top the list of medications we collectively consume. In many cases these medications are helpful. To see if one of them may be right for you, consult your personal physician. Do not order any of them via an online pharmacy. These medications are powerful and some of them can have significantly negative side effects. In a small percentage of individuals, for example, some antidepressants can trigger suicidal thoughts or severe agitation. And if taken in strong doses over a prolonged period of time, some anti-anxiety medications can lead to dependence.

There is no reason that you should not consult with your personal physician or other health-care provider to discuss your scores on the above questionnaires, whether your health care provider agrees with your conclusion, and whether or not a trial on medication would relieve tension. Generally speaking, these medications are safe. Side effects from antidepressants appear more or less right away and can be dealt with by stopping them and then talking with the professional who prescribed them. It's important for you to know that having a negative side effect to one medication does not necessarily mean that you will react in kind to other medications. Stopping one antidepressant and switching to another, for example, may work perfectly well. Similarly, modifying the dosage you are taking to get the effect you want while minimizing negative side effects is also possible. You'll need to work with the person who is prescribing for you to get this done.

As useful as modern mood-altering medications can be, research tells us that they work best if used in conjunction with some counseling. This need not be weekly (though it might be, especially at first, depending on just how severe your anxiety or depression is), but can be spaced out to every other week or every three weeks. The goal of counseling should be for you to come out of each session with some idea of specific things you can do between sessions to help reduce depression and/or anxiety. Here are a few examples:

- *Exercise.*
  Research has shown that a regimen of regular exercise significantly increases the effectiveness of medications for anxiety and depression. This does not even have to be particularly strenuous exercise. Using a treadmill for fifteen minutes a day, or walking a mile at a brisk pace two or three times a week, will gradually build up your metabolism and help medications work more effectively.
- *Diet.*
  Try to minimize the amount of sugar and caffeine you consume. Many snack foods are loaded with ingredients that can give you a fast high, but that soon leave you craving for more. The appeal of these snacks lies in that warm feeling they initially produce. The downside to them is that crash that follows the sugar high, plus the weight you may very well put on.
- *Balance Your Lifestyle.*
  This is the subject of the next chapter. It is so important to parents who are facing divorce that it is worth its status as a topic in and of itself.

Chapter 8

How Balanced is Your Lifestyle?

Divorce, like any life crisis, has the potential to seriously disrupt not only children's lives but their parents' lives as well. Your life may feel precarious and uncertain for a few months or years, and this may prove extremely stressful.

Overcoming anxiety and depression is in your best interest, as well as in your children's best interest. Medication, exercise, and diet can all play a role in this. However, reestablishing some balance in a lifestyle that has gone off kilter is also very important.

After you do the following exercise you might react similarly to a disproportionate number of divorcing parents, who say: "*I didn't realize just how much my life has changed!*" In other words, filling in the pie—dividing your life into slices—can bring into focus just how much divorce can throw a life out of balance. Of course, no one's life is ever divided exactly as they'd like it to be. Many divorcing parents report that the divorce has thrown their lives severely out of balance.

There is a correlation between just how out of balance a person's lifestyle is and how vulnerable they are to experiencing anxiety and depression. If your score on either the Anxiety Inventory or the Depression Inventory from the last chapter is 50 or higher, one contributing factor could be that your life has gotten seriously out of balance. The following questions are questions to consider:

- Which aspects of your lifestyle (pieces of the pie) have grown the most as a result of your divorce?
- Which aspects of your lifestyle have suffered the most?

Your Life as a Pie Chart

Time is the bogeyman of single parents. Often you are working full time, rushing home to pick up your child from school and then rushing through the night to get everything done for the next day. Your life is so full that it is hard to think of the day's elements as falling into discrete spaces. But we all have ways that we can manage our schedule. Think about how you spend your time and divide it into pieces:

1. Think of all the waking hours you have in a given week. Let that total equal 100 percent of the pie.
2. Divide the pie below into slices that represent what proportion of your time *over a week* is devoted to each of the following. Again, the combined total of all your individual slices should be 100 percent:

- Work   _____%
- Family (parents, siblings, etc.)   _____%
- Household chores (cooking, laundry,
  food shopping, cleaning, etc.)   _____%
- Friends   _____%
- Exercise   _____%
- Parenting   _____%
- Relationship (with a significant other)   _____%
- Hobbies   _____%

Total = 100%

- Has the amount of time you devote to parenting been affected by your divorce? If so, how?
- If you were able to get some help, how would you restructure your pie chart to add more balance to your lifestyle?

As many people have told me, knowing your life is out of balance is one thing, but correcting that imbalance is another. This is certainly true. However, doing nothing at all will probably only perpetuate the stress that an out-of-balance lifestyle creates. That is why I have included the last question on the pie chart questionnaire: It is intended to get you thinking about how you might begin to realign your lifestyle.

The best way to start is small, and the best place to start is in that slice of the pie that seems to be the smallest. Typically, parents going through a divorce will sacrifice any personal time they may have had in order to be with their children. Time with friends, time for recreation, and even time with extended family, may drop to virtually zero. Although understandable, this is not acceptable. As time (and the divorce process) wears on, you will most certainly exhaust your strength if this situation remains unchanged. So start to reestablish even a little bit of balance by making a little time for exercise, recreation, and friends. This does not have to be a lot of time, and it does not have to be every day. For example, you might arrange for a sitter to watch the children for a couple of hours so you can meet friends for a meal and conversation. Or, you might sign up at a sports club that has childcare on premises. While these are not dramatic changes, they are changes in the right direction, and if you stick with them they can definitely make a difference over the long run.

A bigger issue might be your reluctance to make time for yourself. You are not alone; most people have a hard time making time for themselves during a divorce, believing that they need to dedicate themselves one hundred percent to their children. One last word on this topic: Some parents have said that they feel they are somehow being selfish, or neglecting their parental responsibilities, if they carve out any time at all in the lives for themselves. There is no good reason for such guilt. We are not talking about oodles of time here. Moreover, some personal time might be taken after the children are asleep, or when they are at some activity. Keep in mind that by at least taking care of the "basic maintenance" on yourself you are keeping yourself in good psychological shape. That in turn will help give you the energy you need to see your child safely though these years.

Chapter 9

Healthy versus Unhealthy Ways of Relieving Your Stress

A Close Call

Laura was a healthcare professional with over 15 years' experience helping patients in a variety of hospital settings. Starting off as what is called a floor nurse in a general medical unit, over the years she had pursued further training and education in a variety of skills and was currently working as an operating room (OR) nurse. She found the job fast-paced and stressful at times, but also very rewarding. In addition to her nursing skills, she had excellent interpersonal skills and was known as one of the OR's most capable staff member when it came to calming an anxious patient, both before and after surgery.

Laura's husband's announcement that he'd fallen in love with another woman and wanted a divorce came as a total surprise to her. Not only had they not been fighting, but she actually thought that their relationship had improved in the past year. Only later did she learn that the "extra hours" her husband was supposedly putting in at work was in fact time spent with this other woman. And it pained Laura to think that if he had seemed happier it wasn't because of her.

Although she had never been much of a drinker, after her husband's abrupt departure, Laura found herself enjoying a glass or two of wine at night. She waited for her two young children to go to bed, which some nights was quite late as they were both upset over their father being gone. She would sit in a recliner in the family room, watch the evening news, and sip her wine along with a light supper.

Laura was not aware that she was slipping into a depression. That's because, as is true for many people, it was a gradual slide, not a precipitous fall. However, seven months after her husband left, Laura had lost nearly twenty pounds. She was sleeping five or six hours a night at most. Moreover, she was now drinking more than half a bottle of wine a night. If her friends asked her how she was doing she would always say that she was fine; but it was obvious that she was not fine at all, or they wouldn't be asking as often as they did.

Finally, one of the surgeons Laura worked with pulled her aside after a day's work and confronted her. He pointed out her weight loss, the fact that she seemed to have lost her sense of humor—indeed, even her ability to smile—and that she just didn't seem to relate to the patients as she had always done before. He summed it up by saying: "You're just not the same Laura I've known for the past five years." He then offered to write a prescription for a sleep aid. Laura first demurred, but he persisted, and she finally accepted.

The sleep aid proved effective, but Laura had not told her colleague about how much she was drinking every night. In truth, she was drinking, taking the sleeping pill, and pretty much passing out. This went on for several weeks, until Laura got the scare of her life. It happened in the middle of the night. She awoke, very slowly and sluggishly, to find her eight-year-old daughter virtually pounding on her and yelling something about her brother. In retrospect it seemed to Laura that she had laid there, only half-conscious, for a long time, her daughter shouting at her. Then she snapped to.

Laura wanted to move quickly once she realized that her daughter was alarmed and trying to get her attention, but she couldn't. She did manage to get up and followed her daughter to her son's bedroom, where she found him curled up in his bed, struggling to breathe. The boy had asthma, and although he'd not been symptomatic recently, he was now in the early stages of a croup attack. If left untreated, Laura knew this could prove fatal. She propped her son up in his bed and instructed her daughter to fetch his asthma medication and the nebulizer from the bathroom. While waiting for that to arrive she gave the boy two tabs of an oral medicine that she also had on hand for such emergencies.

Fortunately, Laura's daughter had been able to rouse her in time, and Laura had had the presence of mind to take action that possibly saved her son's life. No sooner was her son safe and sleeping beside her in bed (with her daughter asleep on her other side), did she realize just how serious the situation had been. The next day she contacted the

hospital's employee assistance program and got a referral to a therapist who specialized in working with divorcing parents. She threw her
sleeping pills in the garbage, and poured her remaining wine down the
kitchen drain.

Unhealthy Stress Management

Maintaining some semblance of balance in your life, along with a resilient outlook on life, are effective ways of managing life crises and keeping
stress to a manageable level through a divorce. Many parents, however,
are tempted to turn to less functional ways of alleviating their stress.
Most popular among these are alcohol and prescription drugs.

Right now you might be thinking: *"Wait a minute! Didn't you say,
not many pages ago, that medication might be a way of dealing with anxiety
or depression?"* Yes, I did, and what I'm talking about here is not that,
but rather the tendency to rely too heavily on medication, as opposed
to things like exercise, diet, and a balanced lifestyle, to cope with stress.
The analogy would be the individual who comes to rely on pain medication too much to deal with pain, as opposed to pursuing physical
therapy, relaxation techniques, and other means of pain management.
Pain medication, sleeping pills, and tranquilizers all have their appropriate uses. By the same token, all of these medications have the potential
for abuse and the associated negative consequences; namely addiction.

As for alcohol, it is something that men and women have turned to
for centuries for a variety of reasons. In low doses alcohol acts as a stress
reliever. Mostly everyone can relate to the individual who comes home
from a day at the office and pours a glass of wine, pops open a beer, or
mixes a cocktail. Used at such levels, alcohol has been an effective way
of relieving stress for just about as long as history has been recorded. On
the other hand, downing a six-pack is a simple stress reliever.

Alcohol is a depressant and a disinhibitor. It disinhibits sexual
behavior; unfortunately, it also can disinhibit aggressive behavior, which
accounts for the overwhelming majority of bar fights. People who are shy
will rely on a drink or two to "loosen up" in social situations. Similarly,
people who experience anxiety about sex sometimes use alcohol for similar reasons. In both cases, while it may seem like a bad idea, it is nevertheless something that people do.

Whether it is drugs or alcohol, all addictions follow a similar course.
If you are going through the stress of a divorce, you may be aware that

you drink more, rely more on prescription medications, or both, in order to get through the day or to get to sleep at night. Of course, this does not necessarily mean that you are addicted. Still, to get a better sense of whether your use of alcohol or prescription medication is (or may become) a problem, take a minute or two to complete the following questionnaire.

Dependency Inventory

Instructions: Answer each of the following questions as it applies to you:

1. I drink or use prescription medications for sleep or anxiety more now than I did six months ago: ____Yes   ____No
2. In an average month I spend more money on alcohol or prescription drugs than I did a year ago: ____Yes   ____No
3. I need to drink more or use more medication to relax now than I did six months ago: ____Yes   ____No
4. I find myself thinking during the day about having a drink or taking medication for stress: ____Yes   ____No
5. I find myself worrying that I might be running low on alcohol or my medication: ____Yes   ____No
6. These days I can't really relax unless I have a drink or take some medication: ____Yes   ____No

---

If you answered *yes* to three or more of the above questions, you should think about reducing your use of alcohol or drugs as a means of coping with stress and substituting something else. Consider some of the recommendations made earlier, especially exercise, diet, and creating some balance in your lifestyle. Relaxation techniques, such as meditation and yoga, can also be very effective. You want to avoid relying on alcohol or drugs to cope with the stress you are under. Otherwise, one or both may begin to affect your ability to guide your child successfully through these crucial years.

If you answered *yes* to five or six of the above questions, you, unfortunately, have some initial signs of dependency. To avoid having this progress to true addiction, your best bet right now is to abstain from alcohol and prescription medication. If you are becoming dependent on prescription medication, talk to your doctor or other prescriber about what, if any, medications you might substitute. Some medications for anxiety are less likely to lead to dependency than others. If it is alcohol that is becoming the problem, you might want to seek some professional counseling to get some ideas of other ways to cope.

* * *

Consider yourself one step ahead of parents who are in the same situation that you are in, but who haven't taken this step: Taking a look at yourself to ensure that you remain part of the solution as far as your child is concerned, instead of becoming part of the problem. As a parent, you will find that it is well worth your time to invest some effort into keeping tabs on your own emotional health during this crucial time in your child's life, so that you can remain in a position to provide your children with what they need to get through this divorce not only psychologically unscathed, but potentially even more resilient than they are now.

Part Three

The Three Crucial Years:
Ages One to Five

The most important tasks facing children in infancy and early childhood are the development of healthy *attachments* and *exploration*
of the world around them, including the physical world and the social
world. Initially children will form attachments to parents (or, sometimes, to parent surrogates such as nannies). Later on, if these early
attachments are successful, they will go on to form attachments to others, including a spouse. Attachment, then, including multiple attachments, is a healthy and desirable thing.

Secure attachment, in turn, forms the base from which the child
ventures forth to explore the world. A securely attached child is free
to learn and develop psychomotor and social competencies, including
language.

When we are talking about young children's needs through the
three crucial years, then, these two words should guide your actions as
a parent: *security* and *exploration*. A securely attached child will learn to
climb, for instance, and then report back to you on the results of his or
her explorations. He or she will get to know other young children and
form the beginnings of relationships. And he or she will be curious and
brave.

In contrast, an insecure child will be excessively clingy. She or he
will hesitate to venture far from the parent, and will become easily anxious. Even minor separations are intolerable for the insecure child. As a
result, development—including language development—will move forward at a slower pace. This can happen if the stress of divorce interferes
with this vital developmental process of attachment. In the worst-case
scenario, a failure of attachment can play a causative role later on in such

problems as depression, self-mutilation, and addiction, all of which can appear as early as late childhood and early adolescence.

The infant and toddler's greatest needs are for consistent nurturance, comfort, safety, and parent–child interaction. When they think of infants at risk, most people think about willful or unintentional neglect. However, a parent who materially provides, but who does not interact; or a parent who leaves a child to comfort him- or herself as opposed to offering comfort and solace, may unwittingly increase the chances that their child will be one of those who are at risk for lasting negative consequences. Because they must face the daunting challenge of parenting—while very likely also having to be a breadwinner and cope with the loss of a marriage—it is easy for a divorcing parent to get distracted. You need to be aware, however, of your child's need not only for sustenance but for an ongoing sense of security, a source of comfort in times of distress, as well as frequent parent–child communication.

As a parent, you need to expect and be ready for your child's increased need for solace and comfort through the divorce, as well as the need for increased interaction and parent–child play. This may be difficult as you may feel that you have *less* time for such things now than you did before. But it is vital that you somehow find the time.

Signs that young children are having problems as a result of their parents' divorce include increased clinginess and general fearfulness; delayed language development; disrupted sleep; bed-wetting in a child who was previously potty trained; weight loss; and a tendency to cry easily.

In Part Three we will address this issue of attachment and what you can do to make sure that separation and divorce does not prevent your child from starting off life on a firm footing.

Chapter 10

Separation and Attachment

Attachment is one of the key development tasks facing a young child—children between the ages of birth and five. It happens to be one of those rare psychological terms that speaks for itself. Beginning at or soon after birth, children become "attached" to others and to things. The most common first attachment is to the mother, who is usually the first person to hold, cuddle, and nurture the newborn. However, attachment is not limited to the mother, but can include the infant's father, as well as others who provide comfort and nurturance and who interact with the infant. Separation and divorce hold the potential to undermine or disrupt attachments that are either being formed or have been formed. If that is allowed to happen, the result can be long-term insecurity and a fear of exploring the world. On the other hand, if divorcing parents understand the process of attachment and act in ways to preserve a child's existing attachments while promoting new ones, there is no reason why that child will be harmed as a result of divorce.

If their initial attachments are successful, children will be able to form additional attachments to significant others later on, with peers as well as with other influential adults in their lives, such as babysitters and day-care workers and, even later, teachers and coaches. Many psychologists believe that healthy attachments in childhood set the stage for satisfying, committed adult relationships.

Children also become attached to things, such as stuffed animals and blankets. They use these things as supplemental attachment objects; they represent additional sources of comfort and companionship, particularly when human attachment figures are not readily available. Many parents can attest to the various collections of these objects that children will collect. My own daughter, Maggie, formed a strong attachment to a stuffed kangaroo when she was about five years old. That same kangaroo eventually accompanied her when she went off to college!

One mother expressed concern because after she and her husband separated, her three-year-old son, Tyler, became very attached to a female doll named "Sparkle," who had long dark brown curly hair that sparkled in the light. The mother had originally gotten the doll for her older daughter, who was more or less neutral about it and made no objections when Tyler appropriated it.

Tyler carried Sparkle with him everywhere and would not go to sleep at night unless Sparkle was at his side. His mother's concern was that her son might be ridiculed by other children for carrying a doll. Since this was a real possibility—especially if Tyler remained attached to Sparkle as he got a couple of years older—the mother was advised not to try to substitute another attachment object, but to simply see to it that Sparkle didn't accompany Tyler to the day-care center. Rather, Sparkle was tucked into bed each morning, where she would spend the day waiting for Tyler to return.

Indeed, Tyler maintained his attachment to Sparkle until he was six. Then, for some reason known only to Tyler, Sparkle was retired to a drawer beneath Tyler's bed, and he began sleeping instead with one or more toy soldiers and Star Wars figurines.

It is not unreasonable to assume that Tyler was experiencing some increased anxiety, or insecurity, as a result of his parents' separation and the decreased presence of his father in his life. Young children like Tyler, however, typically cannot put their insecurity into words. Instead, one has to "read" their behavior. They may become increasingly clingy, for example, or need extra time before being able to fall asleep at night. Some may conjure up imaginary "monsters," while still others will regress and start wetting the bed at night. There are two ways to respond to these behaviors—all of which reflect insecurity. The wrong way is to try to ignore them or talk children out of them. *"Don't feel that way"* will not be sufficient to make insecurity go away. Even worse are efforts to shame young children into dropping their insecurity.

The right way for a separated parent to approach insecurity in a young child is, first, to read these behaviors for what they really are: insecurity. They are not attempts to manipulate the parent or get special favors. Rather than trying to ignore a child's insecurity in the hope it will go away, or else resist the child's efforts to get additional comfort, the divorcing parent needs to accept it and provide the increased comfort and attention that the child is asking for through his or her behavior. In the above example, that would mean respecting and allowing Tyler to have his attachment to Sparkle.

* * *

In addition to things, children also form attachments to places. Think about this. When you were a child, did your family vacation in the same place year after year? Was there a space in your home that you especially liked spending time in? Did you like to arrange your bedroom (or your part of it) in any particular way? And would you be upset if anyone changed the way you'd arranged things?

The above are all examples of attachments to places. As adults we sometimes think of this form of attachment as nostalgia: as a simple longing for days gone by. But these attachments are real, not just wistful thinking. The divorced child's attachments to places—her bedroom, for example, as well as her classroom—need to be recognized. While some disruption in such attachments may be unavoidable, there may be ways to minimize them. One mother, for example, helped her four-year-old daughter recreate her old bedroom in the condo they moved into after the divorce. She did this by choosing the same paint colors, the same border, and the same curtains for the new room as were in the old bedroom. She also negotiated with her husband to move a few key pieces of furniture into the condo, so that each bedroom retained some of its original ambience. Finally, because her daughter was attached to a pet goldfish, she bought a second goldfish, along with an exact replica of the small tank it lived in. These efforts were successful in minimizing this girl's anxiety over having to shuttle between two homes—as was required by the shared-parenting agreement that was part of her parents' divorce settlement.

* * *

Attachments to places—like attachments to people and to things—also play a role in creating a secure base from which children explore and learn. For this reason, children usually object to the idea of having to relocate. One six-year-old boy, for example, carted cardboard boxes into his room and proceeded to cut them up with scissors. When asked by his father why he was cutting the boxes, the boy said, simply, "I don't want to move!" Even at six this boy was attempting to preserve what you could call his "base of operations" from being disrupted by his parents' separation.

We will talk more about this issue of having to relocate children as a consequence of separation and divorce. Again, this may not be avoidable. On the other hand, there may be things that you as a parent can do—as in the above example—to mitigate its effects. These include giving children time to prepare for a move, an opportunity to participate in the move, and a chance to claim and decorate their own space in the new home.

Attachment—to people, places, and things—is the most important developmental task of infancy and the toddler years. Secure attachments allow a child to venture into the world, to explore, and to learn. Children who are not allowed to form secure attachments will be anxious and depressed. They will shrink from the world. And as a result, their social and intellectual development will slow down or even stop.

The Keys to Attachment

Studies of infants and young children have shed light on the keys to helping form attachments. The good news is that attachment, like language, is something that emerges naturally from children. As long as the right environmental conditions are present, children will form attachments naturally, just like they naturally learn to speak. Your challenge, as a parent who is facing divorce, is to make sure that the divorce process does not distract you or absorb you so much that your infant or young child lacks the kind of environment that facilitates the formation of healthy attachments.

Here are the three things a parent needs to be able to provide an infant and toddler in order to ensure that a healthy parent–child attachment is formed:

- *Nurturance*
  Nurturance means providing food, but it also means providing comfort and solace. It means feeding, but it also means cuddling and soothing.
- *Security*
  Security means protecting your child from unnecessary risks, thereby allowing your child to explore the world in safety. It does

not mean overprotecting your child so as to extinguish his or her curiosity. It means providing proper clothing, making sure the environment is free of dangerous objects, and providing appropriate supervision.

- *Interaction*

Interaction includes talking and touching. An infant does not, of course, comprehend the words that are being spoken to him as he is being wheeled through the aisles of a supermarket. But he or she definitely does respond to your tone of voice, to frequent banter, and to your frequent touches and kisses. Similarly, parents of toddlers often notice how their child is a virtual chatterbox who seems to seek continual interaction about everything and anything. An appropriate response to these endless statements can be as simple as "*Okay*" or "*Hmmm.*" These kinds of verbal and physical interactions are what build the parent–child bond, just as surely as nurturance and security do.

Given the stress that divorce creates, it can be easy for a parent to become emotionally worn down or distracted. That's understandable given all you may have on your plate at this time. Still, despite your most diligent efforts, it is possible to *unintentionally* decrease the amount of nurturance and interaction that you would otherwise provide to your child.

Sometimes parents who are trying to juggle too many things at once can also *unintentionally* fail to properly supervise or assure that their child's environment is safe. The result can be a compromised parent–child attachment. This can lead to serious problems beginning in later childhood. Therefore, it's important to make attachment your priority. For that reason alone I recommend that separated parents reach out as much as possible to others who can assist them in any way with the myriad of things they are facing, so as to allow them to maintain and protect the parent–child attachment as best they can. Children can certainly tolerate some dilution in the amount of interaction they have with a parent they are attached to, but this definitely has its limits. When it is stretched too thin you will know it—because some of the signs of *insecurity* that will be discussed shortly will begin to rear their heads.

The following guidelines can be used to help you make sure that attachment moves along despite the stress of your divorce. I recommend that you make a list of all of the following and place it somewhere in your home where you can refer to it on a daily basis. Think of it as a way of "checking in" to make sure that you are providing your child with the tools that she or he needs to become securely attached.

The Importance of Talking

Fathers, more than mothers, are sometimes reluctant to engage infants and young children in talking. Usually, they say, this is because they know that the infant can't understand them. But it is the interaction itself, not the meaning of the words, that promotes parent–child attachment. Therefore, whether it makes sense to you or not, try modeling your behavior on those parents you see talking to even the youngest infants. Try repeating the same phrases over and over, like "*What a good boy!*" of "*What a happy girl you are!*" Your infant's smile, cooing, or body movements in response are your cue that bonding is taking place.

In contrast to infants, toddlers will ramble incessantly about all sorts of things, often changing subjects literally in mid-sentence. Again, finishing a conversation with a toddler is less important than being willing to engage in banter about anything. Often you will need to do little more than nod and mumble a response, or answer a simple question like "*How do you spell hat?*" or "*What is that?*" A lot of the time you simply need to acknowledge that your toddler is saying something to you. Usually, if you listen closely, you will discover that their communication is akin to an ongoing commentary on what they are experiencing or thinking about at the moment. This window onto the world of the toddler can actually be quite enlightening as you witness the steady growth of their intellect and vocabulary. You will discover that your son or daughter suddenly has added a word to their vocabulary that you had no idea they'd even heard before.

Cuddling

Psychologically healthy children love to cuddle. In fact, resistance to cuddling among infants and very young children is cause for concern. It means that something is awry—that for some reason they are having trouble establishing attachments. Assuming this does not describe your child, one thing you can do to facilitate the bonding process is to make time, regularly and often, for cuddling. I recommend you consider the following:

- *Scheduled cuddling time.* Make time in your busy schedule, every day, for 10 to 20 minutes of cuddling time. Sit your infant or toddler in your lap, or up against you, on a comfortable couch or chair. Make sure a comforting blanket is available (even in the summer!). You can spend this time talking, looking at the pictures in a book, reading, or even watching a kids' show on TV. If you do watch television together, make sure that the content of the show you select is age-appropriate. Most shows follow the same rating system used for movies. Try to choose something that makes your child laugh or otherwise respond out loud. The main point here is to create an activity that allows for physical contact that is close and comforting.
- *Random cuddling.* By "random" I mean spontaneous. The fact is that, whether children are two or ten, seizing the moment to give them a hug is a good thing. Don't be discouraged if older children act as if they are uncomfortable—hug them anyway! With toddlers and younger children, seize on opportunities to sit down beside them, ask how they are doing, and give them a hug. By the same token, do not reject your child's attempts to cuddle. Left to their own devices, children will, at least sometimes, climb up into a parent's lap when they spy them sitting, for example, watching television or reading a magazine.

When a parent gets divorced they will often have to take on roles and responsibilities that were once shared by two people. Infants and toddlers are by nature egocentric, and they have fairly intense needs. These needs can come across as burdensome to the parent who feels overwhelmed at times by all they have to do simply to get through the day. Rest assured, however, that doing the kinds of things described in this chapter will save you a lot of stress later on. If you let the bond between you and your child become diluted, one result will be that you have less influence over him or her later on; on the other hand, the stronger the bond between you the more influence you will have when he or she reaches adolescence.

Nurturing versus Feeding

When they read the word "nurturing," many people think of putting food on the table in front of a toddler, or spooning food into the mouth of an infant. To an extent this is true. But nurturing also goes beyond this. It includes, for example:

- Being sensitive to the foods that your child likes and doesn't like.
- Providing "comfort foods" such as ice cream cones or homemade cookies in times of distress.
- Introducing diversity into a child's diet a little bit at a time.
- Having "special" meals from time to time.
- Incorporating rituals, such as saying grace, into mealtimes.
- Keeping children company while they eat.

Trying to incorporate all of the above into meals takes nurturance a step further than feeding and helps to further solidify the parent–child bond.

Providing Comfort

Infants and young children usually make it pretty obvious when they want comforting: they cry; they climb into your lap (or into your bed!); or they become clingy and fretful. When this need for comforting is not met, two things happen. First, the child becomes more anxious. They may cry louder, or cling harder. They may become sulky or moody. Think of these as "louder" signals that comforting is needed.

However, if these louder signals fall on deaf ears, and if their needs are not met, children will stop seeking comfort and become depressed instead. They may then actually resist affection and reject efforts to comfort them. They will become listless, and may spend time curled up in a fetal position. The last of these represents a child's primitive effort to comfort him- or herself. If that begins to happen, professional assistance may be needed to mend the wound in the parent–child bond. All this can be avoided if you as a parent simply respond to your child's desire to be comforted.

One mother reported that her five-year-old son began coming to her and complaining of what seemed to her to be imaginary "boo-boos" about a month after her husband moved out of the house. Although she often could not even make out the supposed injury, she went with her gut feeling, applied a bandage and gave her son a hug. She could have responded by telling her son that he had no boo-boo and should just go on his way, but if she had done so she would have missed the point: Her child was seeking some extra comforting. By responding to his signals, this mother was strengthening the bond between herself and her child.

Another mother explained how both of her young daughters had taken to coming into her bed in the middle of the night, three or four nights a week, after she and her husband separated. This trend worried her. She'd heard stories about how it was bad to allow children to do this; that they would never return to their own beds, and so on. This is not true. Children may need some coaxing to get back in the habit of sleeping all night in their own beds, but once they overcome the anxiety that is driving them to seek extra comfort, this can almost always be done. This woman's solution was to take a few extra minutes every night to get the girls, who shared a bedroom, tucked in. She had them drink some warm milk about half an hour before going to bed. She read them an extra story, made sure they had their stuffed animals, and went through a bedtime ritual that they made up together. She made sure they always started off the night in their own beds, but never said anything to the effect that they could not come to her bed if they felt a need to. After implementing these changes, she noticed that the girls slowly but surely came into her bed less and less often.

Day Care, Babysitters, and Attachment

To the young child, the world is simultaneously inviting and threatening, a source of curiosity as well as anxiety. That is why they need to know that a safe base is nearby. Most often this safe base will be a parent, but today it increasingly is also a babysitter or a day-care worker. The two-career family is now the norm, not the exception, which means that parents have come to rely more and more on home-based day care and commercial day-care centers to supervise their children while they work. And given the fact that people on average work longer hours today than they did, say, twenty years ago, it is not that unusual for a toddler to be in day care for as long as ten hours a day or more.

Divorcing parents are especially likely to need additional childrearing help in the form of regular babysitters and/or a day-care center. Here are a couple of things to keep in mind when considering this option:

- *Expect attachments to form*
  If you do place your child in day care, or hire a regular babysitter or nanny, you can expect your child to form an attachment to one or more adults besides yourself. This will surely happen so long as these people are regular sources of comfort, interaction, and nurturance. Don't bother feeling jealous when this happens, which is what one mother did when her toddler cried when she came to pick him up and he resisted leaving the day-care worker he'd become attached to. She complained to the day-care center supervisor that the staff member was getting "too close" to her child. The supervisor explained as gently as she could that the center had no intention of replacing any parent–child bond, and that this sort of experience was common. That is true, and it is by and large a good thing. Infants and children are capable of multiple attachments. An additional attachment does not represent a threat to the parent–child bond.

- *Be prepared for broken attachments*
  The more worrisome issue that you may have to deal with when placing your child in day care is not that an attachment will form, but that it will be broken. This may be less likely to happen if your child is in a licensed home-based day care operated by one person, perhaps with some additional staff. In that case at least the primary provider is likely to remain there. In contrast, children who are placed in commercial day-care centers often have to deal with a series of broken attachments as they move from one age group to another and staff does not move with them. This does not have to lead to serious or permanent effects, but neither should it be ignored. Day-care centers, unfortunately, are often reluctant to acknowledge just how important staff–child attachments are, and how a child can experience anxiety and depression when that attachment is broken. Staff turnover in commercial day-care centers tends to be high, and children tend to be moved on to new staff every year. Between those two realities, broken attachments are to be expected. The more time your child spends in day care, the more likely it is that he or she will

form an attachment to one or more staff there; consequently, the more difficult any separation will be. When possible, you should plan ahead for such changes. I recommend that you make your child aware of any impending staffing changes ahead of time, so that they at least do not come as a surprise. If your child is old enough, help him or her make one or more good-bye gifts for the departing staff person. Finally, see if you can arrange for your child to maintain at least a little contact with staff that he or she has formed attachments to, even after your child has had to move on with peers to a group that is supervised by a different set of staff.

Play Time

The one form of parent–child interaction that most often falls by the wayside when parents separate is play. When both parents are holding down full-time jobs, in addition to taking on double-duties as a result of a shared-parenting arrangement, it is easy to think of play as either superfluous or something that children can do just fine by themselves, without any parent involvement. "It's okay for my son to spend his time playing, but I don't have time for that," one separated father told me.

However, if you think of play as the equivalent of *work* for a child, it may make sense to join in sometimes. Moreover, playing with your child requires little more than either joining him or her in whatever he or she is already actively engaged in, or else suggesting some simple play activity.

It's no secret that children love to play. Yet what may seem like idle fun when viewed through the eyes of a parent is in fact a child's way of building skills. Play affords opportunities to practice language, to improve psychomotor skills, and, as they get older, to develop conceptual thinking. Evidence for this is easy to see. Beginning in infancy, a child's play includes an element of *challenge*. The infant will reach for things, then manipulate them and stare at them. Similarly, a toddler will play "fill-and-dump" with a pail and blocks (or any suitable substitute) for a long time, in the process building his or her psychomotor skills. And on playgrounds everywhere children are continually challenging themselves on playscapes to accomplish more and more.

Guidelines for Parent–Child Play

Joining your child in play provides you with an opportunity to facilitate development in several ways. Here are some guidelines to follow:

1. In general, let your child select the play activity, rather having it selected for them. This includes letting your child make up games, as well as the rules to go with them. Similarly, on the playground, let your child take the lead in what he or she wants to do.
2. Use the opportunity to encourage your child and to praise your child, for example, when he or she succeeds in making something, wins at a game, or perseveres at a challenge on the playground.
3. Think of your role in play as part cheerleader and part coach. When opportunities arise, provide your child with gentle guidance and advice that helps them do better at whatever they are doing.
4. Avoid criticizing or being overly instructive during play time. You can usually tell when children are feeling overly coached—they will frown or otherwise let their feelings be known, or they will quit the activity.

Using Play to Cement the Parent–Child Bond

Separation and divorce inevitably mean some dilution of each parent–child relationship. It is also a fact that not all parent–child attachments are equally strong at the time that parents separate. Some divorces lead to a shared-parenting arrangement, in which a child spends approximately fifty percent of his or her time with each parent. In these cases, unless each parent has been equally involved in parenting up until that time, there is some chance that shared parenting will lead to the child's increased anxiety as a result of a lessening of his or her primary attachment.

As is true for any other attachment—be it to a parent, a room, or a doll—the correct strategy for dealing with insecurity that is a natural consequence of divorce is not to ignore it or misinterpret it (e.g., as being "spoiled"), but to respect it and do what is within reason to promote healthy attachments. All of the activities discussed in this chapter are useful for separated parents. Rather that being angry at one another, for instance, over a shared-parenting agreement that one of you believes is unfair, better to focus on maintaining and building the bond that each of you already has with your child. Play is an especially easy and fun way to do this. Remember, young children speak through their behavior more than they do through their words. Similarly, telling your child that you love her is good, but spending half an hour interacting and having fun together is another way of saying "*I love you*," and one that also builds the bond between you.

Chapter 11

The Need for Exploration

To ensure that your infant or toddler remains on a healthy developmental track while you work your way through the perils of a divorce, one thing to keep in mind is your child's ongoing need for *exploration*. It is through exploring the world around them and testing themselves that children develop cognitively, physically, and socially. Exploration in turn leads inevitably to challenges. Every time a child overcomes a challenge—from rolling over on his or her stomach in the crib to making a varsity team or getting accepted into that competitive college—he or she builds self-confidence.

Although a child's drive to explore is something that he or she is born with, it can definitely be influenced by outside factors. One of those factors is anxiety. If a child is feeling anxious, the desire to explore can take a back seat to the need for security. Rather than venturing out, the anxious child will instead tend to cling to home base—which is you.

Divorce is one obvious source of anxiety for a child. Despite the fact that a young child cannot intellectually comprehend the true meaning of divorce, that child will nevertheless respond to changes in the environment, as well as to increased stress levels in his or her parents. Children are remarkably accurate readers of their parents' emotional states. When placed in a strange situation, for example, young children will look at their parent's facial expression and take it as a cue whether to feel anxious or relaxed.

Routines are often disrupted, and new ones initiated, when parents make a decision to divorce. The child who was being taken care of by a stay-at-home mother, for example, may suddenly be placed in full-time day care. Parent–child time that was once plentiful may suddenly become scarce. And no matter how hard you may try to conceal it, a child will perceive it when you yourself are feeling worried, depressed, or stressed.

Though it is impossible to totally shield children from stress, or prevent them from experiencing any anxiety as a result of divorce, you can do a lot to minimize any negative effects by being prepared for it, and also by doing what you can to encourage the process of exploration to continue. Successfully overcoming distress, frustration, and anxiety will actually build your child's resilience and put him or her in a better position to deal with future crises should they occur. With your help your child can do this.

Supervising versus Smothering

Understandably, parents may become even more concerned than usual about infant or toddler's well-being during a time of separation and divorce. As a result, they may become more vigilant and protective. In the process, they may unintentionally become somewhat smothering and thereby discourage their child's active need for exploration. Let's look at how you can avoid falling into that trap.

Not all children have an equal need to explore and to test themselves. In order to get a sense for how strong your child's need for exploration is, I suggest you use the following "Playground Test."

The Playground Test

To use the playground test all you have to do is be willing to take your child to a playground, preferably with a friend. Ideally you should pick a time when there are plenty of children on the playground. You will need the friend so that someone else can help keep an eye on your child while you spend some time observing not only your own child but other children.

As you watch the other children, keep an eye out for the following things:

1. Most children appear to challenge themselves to try new things.
2. Some children will repeat the same activity over and over again in an attempt to get better at it.
3. Some children seem to really push themselves to the limit, while others appear to be more cautious.

4. No one has to actively encourage the children to do these things—their motivation comes from within.

The next thing to do is to see where your child fits into the above scheme of things. As you observe your child on the playground, answer the following questions:

1. Does your child show a spontaneous desire to explore?
2. Does your child tend to wander away from you, or stay fairly close?
3. How much does your child appear to push him- or herself to the limits of his or her ability?
4. Does your child repeat activities in an apparent attempt to get better at them?

Third and last, ask yourself the following questions:

1. How comfortable am I with my child's exploration? Does it make me happy, or anxious?
2. How often do I feel the need to intervene so as to keep my child safe?
3. Do I wish my child was more of an explorer and limit-tester?
4. Do I wish my child was less of an explorer and limit-tester?
5. As a child, how would I have compared to my child?

One father who took the playground test was surprised to see just how much of a "daredevil" his seven-year-old son was, especially as compared to the other boys he observed who seemed to be about the same age. "Jude would go right to these bars that he'd have to swing from—a set of eight of them—and keep at it, no matter how many times he'd let go and fall down into the sand in the middle of it, until he was able to get all the way across. He'd swing his body and grab onto one bar after another. The other boys also tried this, but none of them was so determined to finish it." Clearly, this father's son had a strong desire to master physical challenges and was prepared to persevere in the face of failure until he succeeded. As well as he thought he knew his son, it was not until he did this playground test that he realized just how strong a part of his son's personality this was. At home he'd just come to think of his son as stubborn and headstrong, but now he could see this quality in a different light. "I actually admire this about him," the father said.

Self-Efficacy

As children challenge themselves—for example, on a playground—and succeed in achieving their goals, they build what psychologists call *self-efficacy,* which is commonly known as *self-confidence.* Both refer to an individual's inner sense that he or she can succeed, through a combination of perseverance and creativity, in the face of frustration and difficulty. Self-efficacy relates to *resilience* as it is discussed in this book. Resilient people have a clear sense of self-efficacy. Insecure, anxious, and psychologically *fragile* people, in contrast, are apt to give up easily in the face of frustration and turn to others to achieve their goals.

Self-efficacy extends across all the spheres of a person's life, and just because a person may have a strong sense of self-efficacy in one sphere—sports, for example—does not necessarily mean that he or she will have a similar sense of self-efficacy in another sphere, such as academics. On the other hand, children with a good sense of self-efficacy in one sphere can usually be coached to persist and succeed in another if they are given the right combination of encouragement and support.

Of course, there are times when it is perfectly appropriate, indeed desirable, for a child or adult to turn to others for help. But that is not what we mean by self-efficacy. Self-confident people may very well know when to seek help, but they will first attempt to achieve a goal through effort, creativity, and perseverance.

Parents who are overly critical of their children tend to undermine self-efficacy. One father of an athletically talented son was relentlessly critical of his son's performance in hockey and basketball. From his point of view this father was only trying to get his son to do better. But that was not how it came across to the boy.

As it turned out, this man treated his wife and two daughters the same way he treated his son. While the girls more or less ignored their father, the boy had a harder time doing so. After his parents divorced, when the boy was in ninth grade, he abruptly quit sports altogether and voiced the opinion that he had no talent for them. Moreover, whenever he would return from a weekend with his father he was clearly depressed. At one point, he confided in a former coach that he wished he were dead. That remark led to some professional counseling that focused on undoing some of the damage the boy's father had done to his son's self-confidence.

Even children with a healthy sense of self-confidence can have that self-confidence rattled by divorce. As is evident in the above example, less self-confident children can become severely depressed. One of your duties as a parent is to monitor your relationship with each of your children to ensure that you are not crossing over the line from constructive coaching to destructive criticism. Most—but not all—parents seem to have reasonable feeling for where this line lies. Often the ones who do not also came from homes where their same-sex parent was overly critical. These parents tend to lack self-confidence. The good news for them is that, by monitoring their relationship with their child, they can avoid repeating this pattern.

Television for Infants and Toddlers: Pros and Cons

I'm including this section because many divorcing parents have told me that, given how much they have to do, it is tempting to allow their young child to spend a lot of time in front of a television, either watching programmed shows or so-called educational DVDs. I have nothing against educational shows, but I also believe that they have distinct limitations when it comes to how much they can really foster a child's development. The best of them can help a little by teaching concepts, from simple concepts like shapes (*"Can you find the two triangles?"*) to more complex concepts like cause-and-effect (*"The tree fell down because…"*).

As entertaining as children's television programs and educational DVDs can be, I recommend allowing infants and toddlers to spend no more than an hour-and-a-half a day watching them. This is not because they can be harmful in and of themselves, but because they can monopolize a child's time and attention. In doing so they absorb time that could be used for other purposes, especially interacting with others and exploration.

I encourage divorcing parents to use the television judiciously. Here are a few suggestions:

- *Use it as a break.* Kids who actively explore the world, challenge themselves, and interact with peers will naturally need to take breaks. An hour in front of a television, watching a favorite

program or DVD, can give them a chance to catch their breath
and recharge their batteries.

- *Use it as a babysitter aid.* Every parent needs a break now and then,
  including the parent who is going through a divorce. In many
  areas babysitters are hard to find these days, and if you don't have
  close friends or family to call on you may find yourself having very
  little time away from the kids. That being the case, it pays to keep
  a good babysitter happy. One way to do this is to make sure you
  have some food on hand for the babysitter, as well as your child
  or children, when you go out. Another good idea is to have either
  a favorite DVD, or a new one you believe the kids will enjoy, on
  hand for these occasions. That makes the television a treat and
  something to look forward to. It can also make the idea of you
  getting out of the house for a few hours less of a big deal to your
  child.

- *Watch together.* Watching a DVD or a television show together—
  and reacting to it together—represents another way of building the
  parent–child bond. If you try it you will see just how much richer
  the experience of watching a show together can be, as opposed to
  letting your child watch television while you busy yourself with
  chores.

Choosing the Right Toys

Toys are the child's equivalent of an adult's toolbox. They are the vehi-
cles through which they build skills and learn about the world around
them. Unfortunately, children are exposed to a multitude of ads, mostly
on television but also through magazines, which are designed to pique
their interest. Meanwhile, parents are tempted by ads that imply that
buying a game console or certain DVDs will help make their child a
genius. My son, when he was a young child, would routinely turn to
me and say, "*Daddy, can I have that for my birthday?*" at least ten times
during a single child-oriented television show. I did not object to the
contents of these programs, but I found myself annoyed at the incessant
ads and the effect they had on my son. I knew very well that these toys
in reality never lived up to the ads that promoted them. In time I found
myself giving him a routine response: "*I'll put it on the list.*" The list, of
course, did not really exist, and I soon realized that my son quickly for-
got about almost every new toy he asked for within minutes of asking

for it. Of course when his birthday rolled around he did get some toys, but obviously only a small fraction of those he'd asked for that were on the fictional "list."

You might find the above technique useful as well. I find it's better not to argue with young children about such things. They are naturally curious, and television ads are designed to appeal to this curiosity. However, it's also true that many of the toys advertised on television have what I call "short lives" when and if children do actually get them. By this I mean that children find them interesting for only a relatively brief period of time. Within a day or two these toys are usually consigned to an ever-growing pile of abandoned toys that can easily clutter even a very large room.

Many parents do give in to what amounts to a child's whim when choosing what toys to buy. And many a divorcing parent will give in to an urge to buy new toys as a means of compensating for what they think their child is losing as a result of the divorce. Nothing, though, could be further from the truth. Toys are no substitute for relationships, and as long as you see to it that your child maintains a communicative and supportive relationship with you, there is no need to compensate by spoiling your child. On the other hand, it is important that you choose toys that will promote your child's interest in learning and developing their cognitive, psychomotor, and social skills. Here are some suggestions:

- *Choose some toys you can play with together.* There are any number of simple board games and puzzles that can be played with toddlers and young children. Taking 15 to 20 minutes a day to engage your child in such play will help to develop his or her cognitive and social skills.
- *Choose building games.* I include here games like LEGOs, which are available in a size suitable for toddlers, as well as other building games aimed at toddlers. In contrast to many of the toys that are advertised on television, children will typically play with these items over and over again and for long periods of time.
- *Don't rely on "educational" videos.* There are many DVDs available that purport to help children develop their cognitive capacities beginning in infancy. There is nothing wrong with allowing infants and toddlers to watch such DVDs; on the other hand, the claim that they will make a child smarter is highly questionable. Moreover, too much reliance on passively watching a television

screen can deprive a young child of opportunities for exploration and social interaction. My advice: Use these sparingly as you would any television program, as described earlier.

- *Avoid video-game consoles.* I refer here to game consoles that connect to your television and allow a child to play any number of computerized games. I will have more to say about these games later, when we talk about older children. As for this youngest age group, I do not recommend that parents even consider purchasing such a console.

Exploring Challenges Together

I encourage parents not to be afraid to pick a toy or game that they believe might be just a little too advanced for their child. Again, because they might fear that their separation has somehow made their son or daughter more emotionally fragile, some parents choose to play it very safe. They then end up choosing toys or games that present no challenge at all.

If you took the playground test described earlier, as well as reflected on your child's behavior in settings that present a challenge, you should have some good idea about just how much your child is willing to push him- or herself in the face of a challenge. My advice: Don't back away from that line. Instead, strive to strike a balance between games and activities that you are sure they can do, those that might present a bit of a challenge, and those that are quite challenging. This last group is something you should not push children into, but can be there when they are ready to give it a whirl.

Also, don't be afraid to approach the challenging toy or game *together* with your child. Rather than getting anxious when you see your child struggling, sit down and work together on the project. Once again, this accomplishes several purposes. It builds the parent–child bond. It helps develop social skills, as you communicate with each other about not only what to do, but share your frustrations along the way. Finally, it helps build your child's ability to persevere in the face of frustration and challenge, while simultaneously developing his or her cognitive skills.

Chapter 12

Divorce and Insecurity

The decision to separate creates a crisis for the family. It is like throwing a stone into the middle of a still pond. It will cause a splash, and that splash will then be followed by a series of waves that will make their way all the way to shore. In this case the "pond" includes parents and children, of course. It also includes, however, extended family and friends. It includes the very fabric of family life. When divorce occurs, every aspect of our lives (and our children's lives) is vulnerable to feeling the effects. Although very young children seem to be the most susceptible to developing insecurity, the material discussed here is relevant to older children as well. Rather than repeat it, however, we can address it now.

Some of the factors that play a role in determining just how much of a crisis separation will create for children include the following:

- *Changes in financial status.*
  In all but a few cases, separation and divorce is a financial disaster for both parents. The net result is a decrease in income due to the fact that the income that once supported a single family must now support two. This does not necessarily have to be a negative for children, as long as their basic needs are taken care of and as long as they can continue to enjoy activities they've been involved in. However, if a parent has to therefore work two jobs instead of one, or if the family goes from a position of financial stability to having to live week to week, children will perceive this and it will make them anxious.
- *Changes in caretaking.*
  Separation often results in a significant change in the amount of day-to-day parent–child interaction and supervision. Infants and

toddlers may be placed in full-time day care, for example, and teens may become latchkey children overnight, getting off the school bus and coming home into an empty house. Increasingly, divorced parents' solution to having to having a full-time job plus a young child is day care. For children who begin kindergarten there are pre- and after-school programs. Sometime these programs are located within the school the child attends; in other cases school buses drop them off at the center. For slightly older children other creative options may be available. One single mother's solution was to arrange for her eight-year-old daughter to be dropped off at the local library for an hour every day after school. This youngster loved being in the library. She would spend her hour in the children's area, under the watchful eyes of the library staff, first doing her homework and then reading a book or doing a puzzle. Separated parents can find it a challenge to find similar solutions to the issue of supervising their children following separation.

- *Changes in routine.*

Structure and routine provide the "base" from which children and teens venture forth, grow, and learn. To some extent adults also rely on routines. Think of the last time your daily routine was seriously disrupted. How did you react? Chances are the disruption caused you at least some angst. The same is true for your child.

Children, like adults, are adaptable, and they can adjust to changes. However, the more severely children's routines are disrupted, and the more often they are disrupted, the more anxious they will be.

- *Changes in location* (where they live, what school they attend).

Having to move and change schools are among the greatest stressors that a child can face. Researchers, for example, have found a correlation between the number of times children have to change residences and their risk for depression. As many as 50 percent of children who had to relocate more than three times were found to be at risk for severe depression, including suicide attempts.

For children, relocating often means having to make new friends, establish themselves in a new school, and leave old friends. I have spoken with adults who had to do that more than twice when they were children, and a significant number of those adults reported that after the second move they more or less became loners, or established few friendships.

Parents who agree on a shared-parenting arrangement during separation would do well to minimize serious disruptions with respect to their children's schools or established peer groups. Typically, children will say that they prefer to spend more time with the parent whose home happens to be closer to their friends. It is a mistake to react to such requests as if they were statements of rejection. It is also a mistake to try to lure a child to spend more time in the other parent's home by loading it down with more toys and games, for example. Rather, a child-centered approach to divorce recognizes and respects a child's desire to minimize disruptions in his or her lifestyle.

- *Changes in parent–child relationships.*

It goes without saying that separation and divorce will affect a child's relationship with both parents. Shared parenting, for example, often leads to an increase in the intensity of the relationship with one parent, and a simultaneous decrease in the intensity of the relationship with the other parent. Children adjust to such changes best if each parent is able to preserve some key aspects of the parent–child relationship. For example, one father and his twelve-year-old son had established a longstanding ritual of going together once a month to an establishment that featured model car slot racing. They had built three such model cars together, and they were known as "regulars" at this place. In this case, even though this boy was to spend some of these weekends with his mother, she was flexible and child-centered enough to allow her son and ex-husband to continue their ritual without interference.

* * *

Children have an innate drive to explore and test themselves, but this drive is balanced by a need for a stable, predictable lifestyle, along with a secure base from which to venture forth into the world. That base is the parent–child bond, plus a safe environment and regular routines. Toddlers respond to significant changes in this environment with *insecurity*, and as a result they seek comfort. The rule of thumb is this: The more disruptive and unpredictable the change is, the greater the insecurity will be, and therefore the greater the need for comfort.

Sometimes parents feel guilty when their child starts showing signs of insecurity. Some react by trying to more or less talk their child out of feeling the way they do. *"There's nothing to be afraid of,"* they may say when a child suddenly starts saying that he or she is afraid of the dark. Or, they may try to gently push a clingy child away in the belief that such behavior is "immature" or "babyish" and should not be encouraged. This regression is natural and it should not be rejected, because that is likely to make it worse, not better. Similarly, simply telling a child (or an adult for that matter) not to be afraid is not likely to eliminate their anxiety.

As a divorcing parent you should not overreact to an increased need for comforting on the part of your child or children during a divorce; rather, you should anticipate and plan for it.

Dealing with a child's insecurity can be a challenge for a parent who may also be facing major lifestyle changes. Often, divorcing parents will say that time is their scarcest resource (the second is often money). Therefore, what we will look at in this chapter are simple yet effective ways that you can approach this challenge of effective comforting during a divorce.

Signs of Insecurity in Children

Given that it is unrealistic to expect that your child will not be disrupted at all as a result of your divorce, it can be helpful to know what some of the most common signs of insecurity in young children are. They include:

- *Bedwetting,* especially in a child who previously had pretty much gotten beyond this stage.
- *Fear of the dark,* again, especially in a child who has not expressed such fears before.
- *Fear of places,* such as a child's own bedroom or another place in the home.
- *Clinginess,* or a tendency to want to be almost glued to a parent's side.
- *Frequent "boo-boos,"* meaning minor bruises, falls, or other injuries that the child seeks attention and treatment for.
- *Disturbed sleep,* either problems getting to sleep, or getting up in the middle of the night and climbing into the parent's bed.

- *Meltdowns,* or a tendency to cry seemingly at the drop of a hat or in response to a minor frustration or change in routine. Dealing with meltdowns will be covered in more detail later on.

If your child begins to exhibit one or more of the above behaviors, you are pretty safe to conclude that these are expressions of the anxiety over the new social and family context. Insecurity is the common denominator that connects all of these behaviors. It is also common when parents separate, and is more likely the greater the disruption that separation creates.

All of these behaviors can also cause you as a parent to experience a great deal of stress; they can even be annoying. However, it is important that you interpret them as if your child were saying to you, *"I'm anxious,"* and to respond accordingly. What follows are some concrete suggestions for doing so.

The "Band-Aid Cure" for Physical (and Emotional) "Boo-Boos"

Have you ever noticed how children sometimes enjoy wearing bandages, almost as if they were decorations? This is especially true if you give them a colorful bandage for example, or one with a picture of Spiderman or a Disney Princess on it. I routinely advise parents of young children to have an ample supply of such bandages on hand and to use them liberally to soothe all sorts of injuries, including injuries that may be hard (or impossible) to see.

There are times, of course, when a Band-Aid is genuinely needed. Scrapes and small cuts, for example, need to be cleaned and then covered. But there are also those injuries that are so miniscule that one has to wonder if a bandage is really necessary. My advice to parents is this: If the child wants one; give it to him. When children are experiencing stress or anxiety—as they inevitably will, at least at times, as you go through your divorce—they often do something that psychologists refer to as "somaticizing." In other words, they find a physical cause for their distress. This physical cause can be something as simple as bumping up against a piece of furniture, or stepping on a toy in their stocking feet. Rather than dismissing such complaints, I encourage you to minister to them with a ready Band-Aid and a kiss. In doing so you will be offering comfort and solace, not only for the alleged boo-boo, but also for any distress that may lie beneath it.

Dealing with "Bed Phobia"

"Bed phobia" refers to a child's sudden resistance to either falling asleep in his or her own bed, or else refusing to remain there all night. This subject has been touched on but it is worth a few more words since it is probably the most common problem that divorcing parents report having to deal with. Also, dealing with bed phobia can lead to a great deal more stress, for children and parents alike.

Bed phobia usually starts with a child coming into the parent's bed in the middle of the night. At the same time the child may begin having trouble falling asleep in his or her own bed, or may only fall asleep if the parent also sleeps in the bed. Naturally, all of these alternatives can result in a lot of lost sleep and added stress for a parent.

In my observation parents are inclined to worry excessively about bed phobia. They can even get into a test of wills with their child over it, for example, by insisting the child stay in bed when what the child obviously wants is to cuddle with Mommy or Daddy. The younger your child is, the more likely it is that she or he will seek out this additional comfort and solace during a time of divorce. Your son or daughter will probably not be able to articulate exactly *why* they can't fall asleep or want to crawl into bed with you at 2 A.M. Don't worry yourself about this. They cannot describe their own insecurity or understand it for what it is.

I strongly recommend that you *do not turn bedtime into a battleground*. If she or he will fall asleep in his or her own bed if you lie down for ten or fifteen minutes, so be it. If they fall asleep promptly after crawling in your bed, that's okay too. The only time that you might consider this a problem worth talking to a professional about is if your child has a persistent problem falling asleep even after getting into bed with you. That said, my advice is to gently coax your child to sleeping in his or her own bed instead of sleeping with you.

As an added suggestion to those already offered, consider adding music or "white noise" to your child's room at bedtime. So-called white-noise machines can be purchased via many Internet stores, such as Amazon.com. They are small boxes that sit on the floor. When turned on, they start a fan that creates a soothing sound that blocks out other background sounds. If your child is especially sensitive to background sounds and wakes easily, a white-noise machine might be a valuable aid at bedtime.

An alternative to a white-noise machine would be to purchase an inexpensive CD player along with a CD of soothing bedtime music. The music you select for bedtime should be something that you would find soothing if you were to lie down and close your eyes. Playing such music at a low volume at bedtime can also ease the getting-to-sleep process in an anxious child. Once you settle on a suitable CD, make sure to play the same one every night, rather than changing the music. Children love ritual and repetition, and hearing the same music every night can have a very comforting effect.

As a rule, as insecurity wanes, so does a bed phobia. Usually it will get worse only if you fight it too much. Your goal, naturally, is to have your child be able to sleep soundly in his or her own bed. Unless you purposefully encourage them to do otherwise, this will eventually happen.

Clinginess: Do's and Don'ts

Bed phobia, as described above, is best thought of as another form of clinginess. The tendency of children to want more frequent attention than usual, to stay more or less within sight of a parent, and to get upset if they have to separate from a parent are other forms of clinginess that often emerge in times of family crisis, including divorce.

Children often speak through their behavior even more than they do through words. The best way to interpret the above behaviors is that they are saying *I'm anxious and I need comforting.* Accordingly, the best way to respond is to provide some comfort. At the same time I recommend that you help your child learn to use words. Say something like: "Sounds like you want a hug"; or "I think you want to sit down and cuddle together for a few minutes." In time you want your child to be able to use words to express emotions and needs, and this is good training for that.

It can be more difficult for some parents to respond to clinginess when it comes from boys. Old stereotypes die hard, and the stereotype that boys are emotionally tougher than girls lingers on. Nothing, though, could be further from the truth. Boys are equally if not more emotionally sensitive (and, possibly, more emotionally fragile) than girls. Trying to "toughen up" a boy by rejecting his need for comforting as expressed through clingy behavior—or, worse, ridiculing him for it—runs the risk of creating a deeper and more longstanding insecurity.

In contrast, when a parent responds to insecurity and provides comfort, that need is satisfied and tends to lessen over time.

Here, then, are some ground rules for dealing with clinginess:

- Respond to it by providing comfort. Give your child a hug, or sit down together someplace where you can cuddle for a minute.
- Put words to your child's behavior: "Seems like you want to be close to Mommy."
- Do not reject your child's need for comfort, much less ridicule or belittle him or her for it.
- Once your child's need appears to have been met (i.e., he or she is calm and happy), turn their focus to something else with questions or suggestions such as: "How about a snack?"; "Want to draw some pictures?"; "Let's watch _____"; "Let's read a book together"; "Let's play with your doll"; Let's build something with your LEGOs"; or something similar.
- If your child becomes clingy when it is time for you to go somewhere and another adult (babysitter, family member, etc.) will be watching your child, provide your child with the comfort they are seeking for five to ten minutes and then have your replacement sit on the other side of your child and make the above suggestions.

Dealing with Meltdowns

"Meltdown" is a phrase that is commonly spoken among parents today. It's the same garden-variety tantrum, but children today tend to have busier schedules than earlier generations, and fatigue takes its toll. A child worn out by the day's activities will often break down into tears. Beginning as early as kindergarten, schoolwork is significantly more demanding today than it was for a child's parents and grandparents. The result is that even young children can feel burned out at times.

The most likely times for a meltdown to occur are late afternoons and just before bedtime. Almost all children have occasional meltdowns, but if you are going through a divorce you should expect them to happen more often. Even if your child is doing well and seems happy, you shouldn't lose sight of the fact that he or she (like you) is experiencing a crisis. That stress will be operating as a backdrop to your child's daily activities. At times you may forget that it is there—but it *is* there. If you think about it, the same is probably true for you. You may feel happy and on top of things one minute, only to experience an emotional sag the next.

Meltdowns may be inevitable but they can be reduced if you anticipate them and plan ahead for them. Here are some guidelines for doing so:

- Plan your child's schedule so that there is a break, along with a snack, in the late afternoon an hour or so before dinner. If your child is in school, right after he or she gets home in the afternoon can be an ideal time for such a break. Have them kick back, play with something they like, draw, paint, or even watch a favorite television show for half an hour while they have a snack. Try to avoid snacks with a high sugar content, as this can make meltdowns more likely (and worse). If you are home at that time, take a few minutes to join in and interact with your child at break time. Ask what they did that day at school, who they played with, and anything funny or interesting that happened.
- If your child is in school, have him or her do homework immediately after supper. Keep it to less than half an hour a day for the early grades. Approach this as a joint venture, as opposed to something you expect your child to go off and do alone. Turn off the television during homework time. Let your child know that there will be another chance to have a snack and relax after homework is done.
- Don't be alarmed by meltdowns. Just provide your child with some comfort and nutrition, and wait for the meltdown to pass. Then, as you did with clinginess, redirect your child toward another activity.

One mother of a second grader told a story about how she could tell that her son was on the verge of a meltdown virtually every time. "I can see it in his eyes when I pick him up from day care. He looks distracted, and when I try to interest him in conversation on the way home he doesn't really want to talk. This happens once or twice a week. What I've learned to do is, as soon as we get into the house, I have him take off his shoes and lay back on the couch. I put one of his shows on the television and I get him some milk and cookies. If I can do that within a couple of minutes I can almost always avoid a meltdown where he's in tears and inconsolable for half an hour or longer."

Games and Activities as a Means of Reducing Anxiety

One effective way of reducing anxiety is a technique called redirection, which boils down to distracting your child with some activity, from eating a snack to watching television. This technique will only work, however, with a child who is fairly calm. It is not likely to work while a child is in the middle of a meltdown or a fit of clinginess. So it is important to provide a child with the comfort they are seeking before you attempt to redirect them.

Remember that insecurity breeds anxiety. An anxious child simply cannot see beyond their anxiety and become interested in something else. Even offering them their favorite candy will rarely suffice to calm a child who is in the middle of a meltdown. You need to comfort them first. Games represent a great way to help a child move beyond anxiety once they are initially calmed down. Playing games, doing puzzles, drawing, and other craft activities not only provide children with opportunities to grow cognitively, but are sources of comfort and pleasure.

If your child is showing signs of mild to moderate insecurity, engaging in activities that simply facilitate interaction and bonding can often be enough to solve the problem. One of those activities is game-playing, among other, similar activities.

That said, I highly recommend that you purchase a couple of large plastic containers and keep them stocked with the following:

- *Games:* For toddlers "games" include toys that involve stacking and un-stacking, musical toys, push-and-pull toys, and so on. For young children, very simple games like dominoes are good choices. As children get older, the games you keep on hand should grow with them.
- *Puzzles:* Puzzles are great for entertainment as well for redirecting children's attention. For the youngest children puzzles that have fewer pieces (and larger pieces) are best.
- *Drawing materials:* Included here are crayons and washable markers, along with a supply of paper to draw and paint on.
- *Crafting materials:* Supplies that include child-safe scissors, colored construction paper, glue sticks, tape, and string can be used to create all sorts of interesting projects.

In terms of reducing anxiety, engaging your child in any of the above activities is more effective in the long run than relying on television or videos. It isn't necessary to spend a lot of money on these things. If your budget is tight due to the realities of getting a divorce, you should be aware that perfectly good toys, puzzles, and games can often be bought for very little at consignment stores.

If you do shop at consignment stores, just make sure that all the pieces of a game or puzzle are there. Also, check to see that battery-operated toys work. No one—including your children—will care where you got the items they play with, as long as they look good and work as they should.

Bedwetting

Next to bed phobia, the most troubling symptom of insecurity that can crop up during a divorce is a return to bedwetting. This issue can crop up not only during a divorce, but whenever a parent–child relationship is significantly disrupted. For example, if a child who has previously been at home with his mother is suddenly placed in full-time day care, a return to bedwetting may occur. Similarly, incidents of bedwetting may crop up if a child's father changes jobs and suddenly has to be away from home much more than he once was.

The most important thing to know about bedwetting is that it is not necessarily a sign of some deep and lasting pathology in a child. By and large, bedwetting is a symptom of anxiety and insecurity. As such, it can be counted on to go away once the child's anxiety and insecurity passes. Of course, a child may not be able to verbalize that he or she is feeling anxious.

When dealing with an episode of bedwetting, here are the steps to follow:

1. *Don't panic.* This is the first and foremost rule. If your child senses that you are distraught that she or he has wet the bed that will only pump up his or her anxiety.
2. *Back to diapers.* Purchase a supply of the kind of overnight diapers that you probably once used, and start using them again. If your child objects, or seems embarrassed about this, reassure him or her that this sort of thing "happens to kids now and then," and that

it is nothing for either of you to worry about. Also get a plastic mattress cover to put underneath the regular sheets. That will help keep the mattress from getting ruined.

3. *Empty the bladder before bed.* Make sure your child does not have very much to drink for about an hour before bedtime. Also make sure that the last thing he or she does before climbing into bed at night is to "go potty."

4. *Create a bedtime ritual.* If you don't already have one, make up a ritual that you and your child go through every night at bedtime. Whatever it is, make sure you follow it, exactly, every night. Elements of a bedtime ritual can include, but are not limited to, the following: reading; saying a prayer (or meditation); ritual handshakes; and giving goodnight hugs. Keep in mind that the younger children and toddlers who we are talking about in this chapter will frequently want you to read the same story—*Goodnight Moon* is a good one—over and over again. That will change as your child gets older. Here is an example of a bedtime ritual that one father and his five-year-old son devised between them:

> *Father:* "Who's my best buddy?"
> *Son:* "I am. Who's my best buddy?"
> *Father:* "I am. Who's best friends for life?"
> *Son:* "We are!"
> *The ritual ends with a secret handshake and kisses, then lights out (except for a lava lamp on a dresser that serves as this boy's night light.)*

5. *Never punish, criticize, or demean.* Some parents see bedwetting as immature of "babyish" and may communicate this attitude in an attempt to get their child to "grow up" and stop wetting the bed. This approach will almost certainly make the problem worse. No matter how frustrated you may feel, zip your lip and try your best to keep your feelings to yourself.

6. *Don't bother with "point" or "reward" systems.* I am referring here to so-called behavior modification programs. These usually involve giving children a reward of some kind after they have had a designated number of dry nights. Some therapists advocate putting up some kind of chart and using it to mark off those nights when your child does not wet the bed. Then, if the child gets, say, five check marks, he or she gets some kind of reward. The reason I oppose this approach is that it actually adds a measure of tension to the

whole bedwetting episode. The fact is that a wet bed is its own punishment, just as a dry bed is its own reward. There is no need to add another layer of "success" versus "failure."

7. *Build security.* By engaging your child in the various activities described in this chapter, you will gradually decrease any insecurity he or she may be experiencing, and with that the bedwetting episode will pass.

Summing Up Insecurity

Insecurity, at least in its milder forms, is probably the most common issue that separated parents worry about. By maintaining a child-centered focus on separation and tuning into your child's need for a reasonable amount of predictability and routine in his or her life, separated parents can work together to minimize the kinds of disruptions in a child's lifestyle that cause insecurity.

Chapter 13

Building and Maintaining a Support Network

It's lonely to divorce. You might feel like no matter how bad your relationship with your ex-partner was, at least you once had another adult who had a vested interest in your children. Divorce often places strains on relationships with extended family, who had up until this point been a source of support and may now be less so. For example, a sister-in-law who once could be relied upon to watch your child while you went food shopping might not be so available after a divorce action is filed. Now, when the burden might feel like it is squarely on your shoulders, you are probably thinking about how to maximize your support. It is vital for divorcing parents, who lack the mutual support that marriage affords, to build and maintain a support network.

You are also wise to build a support network regardless of how old your child is. Naturally, the nature of the support network you create will vary depending on the age of your child. Ask any parent of a teen, however, and they will attest to how helpful it can be to have a network of other parents to call upon, not only for help but for support in dealing with a teenager!

The title of this chapter includes the word *maintaining* for a reason. It is not enough to simply establish communication once or twice with others, such as teachers or other parents. Rather, it is important to sustain communication once it is established. By the same token it is important to actively facilitate a child's ongoing involvement in at least one structured activity, be that an art class or a karate class.

The goals of establishing the sort of network that is described here are twofold. First, the support network you build will be there as a resource for you as a parent. Second, this network will be an additional means by which your child's social development can move forward. As the very title of Hillary Clinton's book, *It Takes a Village* suggests, it is not reasonable to expect parents to single-handedly provide everything that children to grow into a psychologically healthy and productive citizens.

What follows is a discussion, along with advice and guidelines, for establishing and maintaining an effective network for you and your child.

Networking with Day-Care and Pre-School Staff

When contemplating building a support network, a good place to start is to look for individuals who already play a significant role in your child's life. At this age that most likely will include day-care staff and administrators. I encourage divorcing parents to let these individuals know about their impending divorce. This may not be easy to do. Some divorcing parents experience a lot of shame about getting divorced. Some find it mildly (or very) embarrassing; while others aren't bothered in the least. Regardless of how you feel about your divorce, here are some guidelines to follow when you talk with day-care staff about it:

- Don't share the reasons why you are getting a divorce. This really is no one's business but yours. The less you reveal about the circumstances of your divorce, the less fodder you provide for any rumor mill.
- Let school personnel know about any interim, as well as final, agreements regarding weekly schedules. For example, where will your child be spending his or her nights? Who besides you may be bringing or picking up your child? Will you be authorizing any additional adults to pick up your child from day care on occasion? At this age your child will most likely have one primary day-care provider, who should be your main contact person. However, because day-care centers have a much higher turnover rate than schools, you should also establish communication with the administrative staff at the day-care center, who will, no doubt, also be familiar with your child.
- Advise day-care staff that you definitely want to know if your child's behavior changes in any significant way. You particularly

want to know as soon as possible if your child becomes noticeably distracted, sullen, angry, or oppositional. Learning the alphabet is the most critical academic goal at this stage of development, and learning to sit in a circle for an activity is a primary social goal. Let the day-care staff know that you want to be informed if your child has more than what they would consider normal ups and downs in either of these areas.

The Pediatrician

At those moments when you find yourself wondering whether or not your child is developing "normally," or whether he or she is suffering some potentially permanent consequences as a result of your divorce, no one can be a better source of comfort and common-sense advice than a good pediatrician. That is why your pediatrician is the next person I encourage you to let know about your divorce.

Think of your child's pediatrician as more than someone to consult when your child has a fever, or to get vaccinations or a yearly flu shot. The yearly check-up is also a good time to raise any questions that have been on your mind about your child's development, not only physically but socially, academically, and cognitively. A good pediatrician will be knowledgeable about developmental norms in all of these areas. Keep in mind that you see your child all the time, but that your pediatrician is monitoring the development of literally hundreds of children. As a result the pediatrician has a pretty refined sense of what could be called normal versus something that you should be concerned about.

As important as your child's annual check-up is, don't wait until then to let the pediatrician know about your divorce. Rather, contact them as soon as the first legal step is taken. A quick phone call will suffice. As with teachers, there is no need to go into detail about the reasons for your divorce.

Keeping in mind that divorce represents a crisis in your child's life no matter how hard you try to minimize it, you can take comfort in sharing your concerns with your child's pediatrician. Again, this physician has no doubt seen many children whose parents are going through a divorce and is good at separating reactions that are more or less to be expected from those that may require intervention. In the latter case, your pediatrician can refer you and your child to appropriate professional resources.

Family and Friends

Another piece of the network you should try to establish is with family and friends, including neighbors if they happen to have any children around the same age as yours. You need to be aware, though, that family, friends, and neighbors are often hesitant to express any concerns for fear of upsetting or even angering you. Therefore, you will need to go out of your way to let them know that you do want to know if they observe any behavior that gives them concern.

If friends or family members do express concern about how your divorce may be affecting your child, here's what to do:

1. Ask them to be as specific as possible in describing what about your child's behavior is worrying them. Don't be defensive; rather, hear them out, and preferably take notes.
2. See whether the problem behavior that others are describing is something you also have noticed. If so, is it something that has appeared since your divorce started? Is it something that concerns you as well?
3. In case of doubt, consult with your child's pediatrician to get some advice as to whether this is something you should be concerned about, and, if so, what to do about it. If the pediatrician wants to see your child, make an appointment.

A second reason to network with family, friends, and neighbors is simply to be able to get a few hours of relief now and then. For example, neighbors who have children in the same age group can work out brief, alternative babysitting arrangements. One divorcing mother of a five-year-old boy worked out an arrangement with her neighbor, who had a son of about the same age and who attended the same school-based day-care center, in which one of them picked up both boys one day a week, brought both to their house, and let them play for a couple of hours and have dinner. This arrangement gave both women about a two-and-a-half hour break every week. The divorcing mother used this time to do food shopping and do a brief workout at home. The neighbor used the time to visit with friends.

Babysitters

A couple of generations ago it seemed that babysitters were easy to find. Today, I am told, the motto is: *Blessed are they who have a reliable babysitter!* So don't feel that you are alone if you find it difficult to find a willing and experienced babysitter. To do so you would be wise to check with friends and family who also have children who need at least occasional babysitting services.

Some parents have told me that, knowing that there were teenagers in their neighborhood, they tried passing word in various ways to see if any of these teens would be good babysitters. One divorcing father related an interesting approach. He used a computer program to design an attractive and colorful one-page flier, copied it, and then took a long walk and placed a copy of the flier in each mailbox in the neighborhood. The flier described the two children who needed occasional babysitting, complete with photos, the number of hours that the babysitter would be needed and about how often, and what the hourly fee would be. He ended up interviewing three prospective babysitters. Over time, two of the three became regulars. Other parents have told me they have had success finding babysitters through their local church or other place of worship.

A relationship between your child and one or two babysitters can, indeed, be a blessing. A regular babysitter can easily become another attachment for your child, as well as a source of respite for you. When developing such a relationship, here are some guidelines to follow:

- *Check references.* This is important. If a potential babysitter tells you they have experience, ask for the names and numbers of the parents and talk to them about their experiences. Find out if the sitter is reliable, how the other parents' children relate to the sitter, and if there have ever been any incidents that concerned these parents. If the sitter you are considering has not had prior experience, be sure to talk with the sitter's parents and ask if you can speak to neighbors or other adults who know the sitter well.
- *Emergency preparedness.* Make sure the babysitter knows exactly what to do in the event of an emergency, such as an injury that is more than a minor scrape.
- *Start off slow and easy.* If this is a new babysitter, pay him or her to come and visit with your child for a couple of hours before you actually leave your child with the babysitter. That way they can begin to establish a relationship. It can also make it easier for the babysitter to break the ice and get comfortable with your child.
- *Look for long-term interest.* Be up-front and let any prospective babysitter know that what you would prefer is someone who was

interested in babysitting on some regular basis over the long haul. Say something like, "I'm really hoping to find someone who has the interest in sitting for my child once every few weeks so I can get out or do some shopping."

- *Avoid babysitter burn-out.* Don't push the babysitter to stay longer or sit more often than she or he seems to feel comfortable with. The babysitter is more apt to make a long-term commitment to you and your child under those circumstances. Ironically it is because they are hard to find that many babysitters feel that they are put upon to commit to more than they really want to. The result? They quickly back away.

- *Pay a fair wage.* As a separated parent you want to create as much stability and predictability in your child's life as your can, in order to counterbalance the upheaval that separating and divorce creates. Establishing a relationship with one or two babysitters who will become "regulars" in your child's life is one way to do this. Obviously, you are more likely to keep a babysitter for a long period of time if you make it worth his or her while. Before you employ a babysitter, ask what she or he expects (or has received in the past) as wages. Also, little "benefits," such as a pizza or snacks and something to drink, can make the babysitting experience more rewarding for both your child and the sitter.

- *Keep your initial outings relatively brief.* Make sure the babysitter knows how to get in touch with you if necessary. A cell phone number is best—and make sure the ringer in on. When you first leave your child with the sitter, limit it to a couple of hours. Then, as time goes on, and the child–sitter relationship gets stronger, you can gradually extend the amount of time you leave them together.

Establishing Your Child's Peer Group

Although true "friendships" will have to wait until your child moves into the next developmental stage, it's not too early to begin the process of establishing a peer group during the toddler years. If you are placing your child in a day-care center in the same town where he or she will be going to school, this process will begin then and there. More and more school systems today offer parents an opportunity to begin this process of socialization through weekly or semi-monthly two-hour "play-time" programs for pre-kindergartners. These programs are usually either free or low cost, and are open to all toddlers who reside in that school district. The purpose of these sessions is to promote children's social development. The reason this is important to schools is that the curriculum in kindergarten has become significantly more rigorous in recent years. To prepare preschoolers (as well as their parents) for this, many school systems now offer a program of periodic play times. These programs offer an opportunity for children who will soon be classmates to meet one another, and also to be exposed to the kinds of activities they will be asked to be part of in kindergarten.

If your child is not in day care, you should definitely sign him or her up for such a program and attend it together. This will give you a window into what will be expected once your child begins kindergarten. You can then start practicing this at home. For example, if the children in the play group are asked to sit in a circle together and listen to a teacher read a story, you can (and should) begin doing this once or twice a week at home. Ask you child to sit beside you, read the story, and then talk about it: *What was the story about? Who was the main character? How did the story end?*

Another advantage of these preschool programs is that you may meet one or two other parents whose children will be your child's classmates. It's a good idea to introduce yourself to these parents. Thinking ahead, you may very well be seeing these parents and their children in the years ahead at birthday parties and play dates.

Support for Parent and Child

Building a support network is not only good for your child, but for you as well. Being a separated parent is already a lonely position to be in; without supporters to pitch in and provide you with a respite now and then, being a single parent can be downright oppressive. By following the suggestions offered in this chapter you will not only be helping to avoid or minimize any insecurity your child might experience as a result of separation, but also providing some opportunities for you to maintain some social contact. For example, I recommend that when it is your child's turn to visit a friend for a play date, you meet a friend for lunch, shopping, or any other activity that helps to keep in touch with friends and family.

Part Four

The Three Crucial Years:
Ages Six to Eleven

The primary developmental goals during the first years of life, as described in Part Three, are attachment and exploration. In later childhood—roughly ages six through eleven—the primary developmental tasks shift to *socialization* and *literacy*. If your child falls within this age group—or will be transitioning into it—during the three crucial years, the material here in Part Four will be very relevant for you.

It is not coincidental that this developmental stage coincides with the start of formal education. Research has demonstrated that children who fall behind academically by third grade are at risk for long-term academic difficulties. The stress of divorce can (but does not have to) negatively impact a child's ability to learn. Aside from academic problems, signs that your separation may be having deleterious effects during these years include school phobia, nightmares, social phobia, temper tantrums, and oppositional behavior in a previously compliant child. This is a critical time for parenting, and the divorcing parent who becomes distracted or incapacitated during this time, for example, through anxiety or depression, may not be in a position to identify warning signs, or to intervene effectively in order to prevent their child from becoming one of the 25 percent of children who will suffer long-term consequences as a result of divorce.

Part Four reviews these key developmental tasks of later childhood. It will educate you on signs to be watchful for, and give you prescriptive advice for how to effectively intervene, if necessary. Again, your goal is not to shield your child from all stress, but to keep your child on a healthy developmental track. As long as he or she remains on such a track, everything will work out just fine. Your child may even emerge from the three crucial years a psychologically stronger individual.

Chapter 14

Guiding your Child toward Healthy Peer Groups

As a parent of a child aged six to eleven, it is important to monitor the peers toward whom your child is gravitating. Remember, too, that parents can be proactive in helping children find appropriate peer groups to identify with—which is preferable to leaving this entirely to chance. The word *groups* is used here intentionally, since it is entirely possible and reasonable to expect children in this age group to have more than one circle of friends that they relate to and interact with.

A firm connection to a functional peer group represents another way of "anchoring" a child in order to ease the stress of separation and divorce. One of the central concerns that children of divorce have, almost immediately on learning that their parents are separating, is whether their circle of friends (and classmates) will be disrupted. If such a peer group already exists, then child-centered divorce demands that parents cooperate so as to preserve it. If it does not exist, facilitating it can go a long way toward helping children navigate their way successfully through the divorce process.

The Play Date

Peer groups are essential components to a child's social network. This network begins to emerge during the toddler years. As children pass into this next developmental stage, however, the social network grows considerably in terms of its importance. The "play date," for example, is a social phenomenon that typically begins between first and third grades, and is often preceded by invitations to birthday parties. You can expect that your child will want to have play dates with peers found wherever it is that your child has the most opportunity for free interaction, or play, with others his or her age: the school classroom, your neighborhood, or church, for example.

Girls seem to be more precocious than boys when it comes to asking for play dates. By age six most girls will express such an interest, usually with their best friends. Boys will typically express this interest a bit later.

It is important that you facilitate play dates, although just how often you do so may depend on factors such as your work schedule and weekend responsibilities. As a rule of thumb, though, once a month is fine.

Play dates promote your child's social development. At the same time they can be a welcome source of relief from the stress that your divorce may be creating.

Here are some guidelines for making play dates:

- *Make sure your son or daughter is really up for it.*
  Although I am definitely in favor of play dates, make sure that the idea comes from your child rather than from you. Chances are your child knows what play dates are from their friends in school or the neighborhood. Wait until your child says, *"Can I ask _____ over for a play date?,"* or *"Can I go to _____'s for a play date?."* Don't be surprised if your child initially wants to go to a friend's house, especially if he or she is the adventurous type, since that represents more of an adventure than having the friend to your house.
- *Talk to the friend's parent in advance to get the okay and set the time.*
  Regardless of who will be visiting whom, contact the parent of your child's friend and discuss the play date. Make sure your own child knows in advance that while you are willing to *ask* about a play date, there is no guarantee that it will happen, for instance, if there are conflicting commitments. Introduce yourself as _____'s parent. Explain that your child wants to have a play date and see what kind of response you get. Most of the time other parents will be aware of their own child's friends and will recognize your child's name, if not yours. Also, be sure to mention the idea of reciprocity.
- *Limit play dates to two to three hours maximum at first.*
  I recommend not leaving the length of first play dates open-ended or too long. As much fun as a play date can be for children, guests

can easily wear out their welcome if the play dates go on too long. Let your child know how long the friend will be visiting and stick to the schedule even if they protest. This is the best way to ensure that future play dates will happen.

- *Plan for a structured activity and a snack.*
  If the play date will be at your home, don't assume that your child and the friend will be able to fill up an entire two or three hours without a little assistance. It's a good idea to think of a structured activity or two in advance and to have them ready, just in case. These can include games, drawing or coloring activities, craft activities, or age-appropriate DVDs. If the play date goes along without any need for assistance from you, you can always put your back-up plan on hold for next time.

  Finally, you should plan on having the children take a short break about halfway through the play date for a snack. It is also important to ask the other parent in advance if the snack you are thinking of offering is okay. Some children have allergies to certain foods, and some parents have certain restrictions on what their children can and cannot eat: for example, sugary snacks.

- *Supervise but don't dictate.*
  This guideline goes along with the previous one. Although you can allow your child and the friend to decide for themselves what to do, don't assume that they can be counted on to successfully get along for two hours or more. Do not allow them to be out of your sight for more than a couple of minutes so that you can supervise the play, especially if they are playing outside. Although this may feel like a bit of a burden, think of what you would expect from another parent if your child were visiting their home.

- *Plan on reciprocating.*
  This may be the best part of play dates. When you first make the call to discuss a play date, make sure you mention this idea of reciprocity. It is good for your child not only to visit a friend's house, but to have that friend visit your house. Let your child know that reciprocity is an integral part of the play-date process and that she or he should plan on it. Then, follow up when the time seems right. Play dates are especially nice things to plan during school breaks and vacations. They can make for a pleasant break in the day as well as events for your child to look forward to.

Daisies, Brownies, and Cub Scouts

One way to steer your child toward a healthy peer group is to make use of established organizations: for example, scouting. For girls, the most popular scouting organization is the Girl Scouts of the USA, which has several programs for different age groups. In kindergarten and first grade, girls can join the Daisies; and from first to third grade, girls can join the Brownies program. The most popular scouting organization for boys is the Boy Scouts of America. For young boys, the starting point in the Boy Scouts is the Cub Scouts (grades one through five). I recommend that you consider at least exposing your son or daughter to one of these organizations, and see what kind of reaction you get. I am not a proponent of forcing or pressuring children to join specific activities. However, I do advocate introducing them to such things, and then facilitating their involvement if they do express an interest.

Organizations like the Boy Scouts and the Girl Scouts are very much kid-centered and offer your child opportunities to make new friends, learn new skills, and experience the feeling of success that comes from achieving specific goals or skills. In the scout organizations, children are rewarded for these achievements with badges. These badges are awarded for performing tasks that are very much geared to a child's developmental level. Some badges are earned through simple participation in an event. For others—from knot-tying to learning how to grow a vegetable from a seed—books are available that guide children step by step. Moreover, parents are encouraged to work with their child on any given task. Badges are typically awarded at group meetings. As an example, the following is a sampling of badges that can be earned by boys who join the Cub Scouts:

- Geology
- Computers
- Citizenship
- Ice Skating
- Bicycling
- Swimming
- Mathematics
- Wildlife Conservation
- Language and Culture

The Girl Scouts offers a similar list of activities for which young girls who are enrolled as Brownies can earn badges. In all cases, parents are strongly encouraged to work together with their child to earn badges, and the organizations publish guidelines for parents to use. Even if a child chooses not to pursue active participation in one of these organizations, these materials can still be used as guides to constructive parent–child activities.

When children find themselves in the midst of a crisis such as divorce, group activities like scouting can be especially helpful. They allow children to build bonds with peers, with other adults, and with parents. Group activities, such as scouting, also give you an opportunity to meet and get to know other parents (some of whom may be a situation like yours). This in turn can set the stage for play dates, as described earlier.

One way to prepare yourself for scouting is to purchase the book that your child will be using and that contains the instructions for earning various badges. Check out the requirements to see if these are things you can do (and would enjoy doing) with your child. It's easy to see how these activities, if done together, can strengthen the parent–child bond. As you will learn shortly, that bond will make correcting and disciplining your child much easier.

Other Structured Social Activities

Your goal as the parent of a child in this age group is to do what you can to steer your child toward healthy peer groups. Besides scouting, as discussed above, you can foster healthy social development by tapping into your child's innate interests, and by exposing them to opportunities to make friends with these shared interests. Some activities that are well worth exploring include the following:

- *Soccer, T-Ball, and Baseball*
  Most towns now sponsor organized soccer, T-ball, and baseball leagues for children ages five and up. Whereas these activities were once separated by sex, today it is more common to see co-ed leagues and teams. Appropriate for younger children, T-ball is a precursor to regular baseball. In T-ball, children are taught to hit a soft ball off the top of a T-shaped rubber cylinder. Rather than

being competitive with formal scoring, the rule in T-ball is that every player gets an at-bat in each of five innings. This means that every child gets to hit and run the bases, and those playing the field get to practice catching (or, at least, stopping) the ball and throwing it.

- *Art, Music, and Drama*

  It's a good idea to balance physical and athletic activities with artistic ones in order to help your child round out his or her interests. These activities can include art classes, music classes, and drama classes. Drama Kids, for example, is a national franchise that offers structured (and fun) activities that teach children basic drama skills such as projecting one's voice, expressing one's self nonverbally, and so on. Children are grouped in Drama Kids classes according to age. Because the activities are designed to be done collectively, and because they are so much fun, this activity can be a very helpful way of helping a shy child overcome that shyness.

  The best ways to locate local art and music programs include your school system and your community newspapers. If you live reasonably close to a college, check them out to see if their art or music departments offer any such programs for children. Again, look for programs that group children by age. Although these will be activities that your child will be involved in without you, they can be very powerful ways of boosting your child's sense of competence and at the same time broaden his or her self-concept.

- *Gymnastics and Karate*

  These group activities have become increasingly popular among children in this age group. Of the two, karate can be the more competitive, as it involves earning belts that require progressively more disciplined abilities. As with sports, today these activities tend to be co-ed. Karate is offered through schools, and you should check several out by asking to observe a class before you sign your child up. As with scouting, it is also best to have your child give karate a try before you commit a sum of money to it. As a rule young girls seem better able than same-age boys to handle the rigor required by karate. Boys, in contrast, often enjoy the drama and action that surrounds karate, but may lack the self-control to advance at it until they are at least eight or nine. Therefore, if you are the parent of a six- or seven-year-old boy, don't feel dismayed if he wants to take karate classes but has a hard time taking direction or paying attention during classes. Rather than having it turn into a frustrating experience, it is better to tell him that you think it best to place karate on hold for a period of time. You can take some of the sting out of such a decision by suggesting an alternative activity, such as gymnastics.

Gymnastics is another group activity that is suitable for children in this age group. Like karate, gymnastics involves a lot of movement. As such, it is a great activity for building strength and agility, while at the same time burning energy. Gymnastics has the potential to be competitive, although gyms that offer gymnastics programs for younger children tend to put the focus on basic skill-building and having fun. As with all the other activities we are discussing here, gymnastics classes offer opportunities for your child to expand his or her peer group and make new friends. If for some reason your divorce has meant that your child has had to leave old friends, these activities are a relatively easy way for a child to make new friends based on common interests.

- *Get-togethers*

I have been impressed over my years of working with families with how creative parents can be in devising group activities that facilitate their children being able to form bonds with a peer group. Here are a few examples of what I call "get-togethers," since they involve not one peer but two or three:

Wizard of Oz Get-Together: The children are told to dress up as best they can as one of the movie characters, and then all the children sit down to watch the movie together. Be sure to serve popcorn and juice! The kids will love to sing along. Make sure you tell them they can close their eyes any time they want to (such as during the flying monkeys scenes!).

Star Wars Get-Together: Same as above, but dressing up as a Star Wars character and watching one of the "G"-rated cartoon versions of the Star Wars adventure series. Again, popcorn and juice!

Gingerbread-House Making: A great holiday theme. Bake gingerbread in advance and cut it into various size pieces. Have frosting and other edible decorative treats available. The children each build a small gingerbread house and decorate it, then take it home.

Cookie-Making Get-Together: Same as above, but easier. All you need is ready-made cookie dough and an assortment of added ingredients such as chocolate chips, M&Ms, tubes of icing, and so on.

LEGO Get-Together: Particularly popular with boys. Keep a theme or two in mind (cars, spaceships), along with plenty of LEGO blocks.

The above get-togethers, as described to me by parents who have hosted them, are not as elaborate as full-fledged "parties" (for example, birthday parties). Rather, they are activities that parents have used as a focus for getting three or four same-age, same-sex children together for the purpose of having fun and building the bonds of friendship.

These get-togethers can be a bit more than some single parents might want to try to pull off alone. If that includes you, you might want to consider asking a friend or family member to come along as extra help. Teenage nieces and nephews are often willing to do this (especially for a few dollars!).

Get-togethers such as the above can really help to boost a child's connection with friends. However, they do not need to happen more than, say, once a year, especially if you also plan on hosting a birthday party that will include friends.

Making Your Home a Peer-Friendly Environment

Another way that you can help to steer your child toward healthy peer groups is to ensure that your home environment is welcoming to young children and is a place your child feels comfortable inviting friends into. Of course, you do not need to convert your living space into a carnival. On the other hand, neither should your living space be stark, cold, or empty—at least not if you want kids to come to play there. Here are some guidelines for making your home a kid-friendly environment:

- *Childproof your play space.*
  Make sure whatever space in your home is designated for play does not contain your most valuable china, precious knickknacks, or anything else that is fragile and valuable. In other words, make it a space that kids can play in without you having to watch over it every second to ensure that nothing gets damaged.
- *Avoid excessive clutter and chaos.*
  Structure and order are not inconsistent with having fun. As any teacher can tell you, children in this age group respond to chaos and disorganization by acting in chaotic and disorganized ways;

conversely, children respond to order and structure with self-control.

- *Have toys and games available but not scattered.*

Appropriate toys for this age group (six through eleven) include puzzles and simple games, building toys, such as LEGOs, dolls and doll clothes, crayons, paper, and glue sticks, toy animals (typically, dinosaurs and the like for boys, horses and the like for girls) as well as "G"-rated movies that your child has seen or wants to see. Do not make these items all available at once, however, or they are likely to quickly turn into one huge mess in the middle of your floor. Also, young children can have a hard time choosing one activity to focus on when an array of different ones are presented to them. Instead, either ask the children what they'd like to do next or ask them to choose between two options, and make one activity at a time available to them. When they are finished with that activity, have them help you put it away and then ask what they want to do next.

- *Have healthy, tasty snacks available—but dole them out yourself.*

If you are a separated parent but have had relatively little past experience organizing and supervising the kinds of activities described here, this can be a very important rule to remember. Kids need snack breaks about every hour and a half. This should include milk or juice along with a reasonably healthy snack that isn't overly loaded with sugar or high-fructose corn syrup, as these ingredients tend to give kids a quick surge of energy that is followed by a crash. As with toys, don't just leave a pile of snacks out and expect children not to take advantage of the opportunity. Instead, when they seem to be at or near the end of an activity (or when roughly an hour and a half has gone by), suggest that they take a break for a snack. This approach mimics what typically goes on in classrooms and your child and his or her friends are no doubt already familiar with it.

- *Invite your child's friends for play dates as described earlier, one at a time.*

Separated parents who are trying to implement a shared parenting agreement but have had less hands-on experience often bite off more than they can chew in their first attempts to promote their children's social contact. Unless you happen to be someone who is adept at coordinating and supervising the activities of several children at a time, you are strongly advised to limit play dates to one friend at a time. The get-togethers described earlier can be a lot of fun. However, they require much more planning than a simple play date. It takes a lot of energy to monitor young children, and chances are you do not have a lot of help right now when it comes to supervising children.

- *Have a couple of structured activities in mind in case the kids seem to get stuck on something to do.*

As noted earlier, an important point to remember in keeping a kid-friendly home is to ensure that structured activities are available when needed. You would be surprised how many parents forget to do this. If your child and his or her playmate happen to be stumped for something to do, and you have not thought ahead of structured activities, you will be stumped as well. Having a few things on hand—an extra puzzle or two, a new game, or a good "G"-rated DVD your child has not yet seen—can save you a lot of stress during a play date that sputters or stalls.

Anticipate Potential Questions

At the outset of this book I made the point that, while your child may be reticent to talk about your separation and divorce with you, one should not assume that this means that your child isn't talking to other children about it. In addition, you should not assume that your child is naïve about divorce. It is a virtual certainty that your child will know several other children whose parents are either divorced or divorcing. They will also know several children who are living in a blended family. The older children get the more they will talk about their living situations and the more problems and conflicts they will disclose to their peers. I witnessed this firsthand when I consulted over a period of six years to a residential treatment and foster care facility for children and adolescents. It was truly remarkable how much these children and teens revealed to one another—about their parents' conflict, substance abuse issues, infidelities, and so on. If these discussions occurred in a relaxed social setting (for example, a soda shop) and if a counselor (like myself) happened to be present, this uninhibited communication continued to flow. It would even be possible to offer comments or ask qualifying questions, such as *"What do you do when your mother starts drinking every night after dinner?"* In contrast, these same children might have little or nothing to say if these same issues were to be brought up in a family counseling session.

The moral of the story, then, is to assume that your child is aware of your personal faults and flaws, and may very well have shared some of this with a friend or friends.

I have come in time to see the above process as an essentially healthy and helpful one. If you consider that we as adults are most likely to seek support and listen to advice offered by people who we perceive as understanding our situation—groups for separated parents, or for single mothers, for example—then it makes sense that children and teens would also seek support and advise from peers whom they perceive as being in the same boat that they are in.

The fact that your child is most likely *not* sitting on a big secret (your separation) can be a comfort. However, it doesn't hurt, especially if your child is very young, to directly ask if any of his friends' parents are separated or divorced. In the unlikely event that the answer is no, you should follow up by asking what your child says if a friend asks about your separation, or if a friend asks about where the other parent is. "What would you say?" you can ask, as well as "Would it bother you if a friend asked you that?"

The other direction from which questions may come your way may be from the parents of your child's friends. My advice is to be straight-forward and not defensive when faced with such questions as "Will your wife be there during the play date?' If you are the separated father of a daughter you may even encounter some resistance to having play dates. As a rule mothers are perceived by most people as more competent than men when it comes to arranging play dates, birthday parties, and so on.

The way to get around any hesitation is to be up front about the plans you have made. If it is for a play date, specify the time it will begin and end. Explain what activity you have planned. And it wouldn't hurt to say what kind of snack you've planned for and ask if that is okay with the other parent. Make sure you exchange cell phone numbers as well. Initiating these kinds of conversations and exchanging this kind of information will be reassuring to other parents.

Chapter 15

The Importance of Structure, Predictability, and Routine

One theme I have laid out in this book is the idea that, in a child-centered divorce, parents make an effort to minimize severe disruptions in a child's lifestyle and at the same time, that they make an effort to make their child's life predictable and structured. Some people are of the opinion that change itself is necessarily detrimental to children, especially the kind of change that separation represents. Yet research suggests that it is not change per se, but rather *unpredictability and chaos,* that are the greater risk factors. Lifestyle change is inevitable for many parents facing divorce, and therefore for their children as well. These include changes in gross income, living accommodations, and disposable income, to name only a few.

The divorcing parent needs to strive not so much to *eliminate* change in their child's life, but rather to *manage* it, and specifically to allow their child to anticipate and plan for such change as much as possible.

Children thrive, developmentally speaking, on routine and predictability. That stability and structure, in turn, sets the stage for them to move forward on the two developmental fronts that are so important at this point in their lives: socialization and literacy. Divorce can be a highly disruptive force. Your goal during these crucial years is to create the kind of environment that will allow your child to stay "on course" developmentally.

Daily Routines

One of the most common comments made by parents who are going through a divorce is how much an effect the divorce has had on their daily and weekly routines. "*My life has been turned upside-down*" is a typical remark. Naturally, this means that not only the parent's life has been turned upside-down, but also the child's.

Children's development tends to follow a natural progression, For example, it is fairly well established that all children will learn to talk within a certain span of time, and that they will also learn to read. Little or no formal instruction is needed to learn speech, but some instruction is needed for a child to become literate. Given how complex learning to read is, it is really a wonder how little instruction most children need, and how much progress slower readers can make with even a modicum of extra help.

Structure, predictability, and stability in day-to-day life is as important as instruction is to learning. This is where the disruptive force of a divorce can lead to academic and social deficits that have a long-term effect on a child. To prevent this, you do not have to become your child's tutor or even put in more time on homework than the average parent would. What you need to do is to insure that your child's life maintains a degree of stability and predictability. What follows are guidelines for doing this. If you think of your child's day as one of those old-fashioned pie charts, a good chunk of the pie will be taken up by two activities: school and sleep. Your job as a parent is to make sure that the activities cited below fit into the pie of your child's life on a regular and consistent basis. They should vary as little as possible from day to day, and they should be as predictable as possible. One way for you to accomplish this is to write out a daily schedule and post it somewhere for everyone to see. Let's go through them one by one:

- *Dinner Time:* Perhaps we should not be surprised, given the way our lifestyles have changed, that even two-parent families often struggle to maintain regular mealtimes. Dinner is the most important meal for families. It may be unrealistic to expect either two parents or a single parent these days to reproduce the sort of dinnertime scenario that was depicted, say, by Norman Rockwell in his famous Americana paintings, with everyone seated around the table, napkins in hand, passing around the meat, vegetables, and potatoes. On the other hand, we do not have to totally give in to chaos, with everyone eating separately, in different places and at different times. That kind of situation is not conducive to a child's healthy development. It can limit social development, since the daily family meal is an opportunity for social interaction. Moreover, a chaotic dinner time tends to be a symptom of a larger chaotic family life, which is detrimental to academic success.

- *Homework Time:* Once children start first grade, you can expect them to have some daily homework. Usually this will involve reading, spelling, and basic arithmetic. You may be asked to help your child read a short book, and then sign a check-off sheet indicating that you have done so. Chances are your child will also bring home one or two handouts to be done as homework every day. The best times to assign as homework times are soon after school (following a break for a snack) or shortly after dinner. If you wait too long after dinner you are apt to run into that time when your child's energy and ability to focus is sapped. Do not hesitate to designate a "homework time" and enforce it by turning off all distractions such as television and music. This typically does not have to be longer than twenty minutes to half an hour, depending on what grade your child is in. It is most important that you personally supervise homework. You don't necessarily have to stand over your child's shoulder, but neither should you be in another room occupied with something else. By the same token, although it may make life less stressful for you, do not allow your child to do his or her homework in bed, or with an MP3 player pumping music into his or her ears. Make sure your child knows you are ready and willing to help with homework, and be sure to check your child's homework every day for completeness and accuracy. Finally, don't hesitate to communicate with teachers about any concerns you have about your child's homework.

- *Play Time:* Play time is as important as homework time, but it should also be monitored. During these years your child's play may include: playing video or computer games, either through a video-game console or by visiting an appropriate, child-oriented website (many of which have free games available); watching television; doing puzzles; drawing and other art work; playing with building toys, dolls, or plastic animals; and reading. All of these activities are fine, but your role as a parent is to be sure that your child's play remains somewhat balanced across these various activities. As a rule, children should play computer or video games for no more than one hour at a time. Also, while you do not have to play with your child all the time, you may find some occasional parent–child play time to be a nice break. Finally, as busy as you may be as a single parent, do not allow your child's play (especially if it involves the Internet) to go unsupervised. Play time is best scheduled for right after school and again after homework time in the evening.

- *Bedtime Rituals:* Bedtime rituals are very important to children. They are a means to "close out" the day and reconnect with you. Chances are, you and your child have already established some bedtime rituals. If so, do not let the distraction of divorce allow you to abandon these. Over time these rituals may evolve and change. You can also invent new ones, such as "secret" hand shakes and pledges. During the first three crucial years of your divorce, rituals like the above can play a vital role in helping your child manage any insecurity he or she may be experiencing. That insecurity tends to come out at night—just when bedtime rituals come in handy. Common elements of bedtime rituals include: reading stories; sharing something interesting or funny that happened that day; saying prayers or meditations; and repeating good-night rituals. If you have more than one child, you may be able to convert some of your bedtime rituals—reading, for example—into something you all do together, to make it a bit more efficient for you. The children's book section in your local library is a good resource for an ongoing supply of age-appropriate bedtime stories.

Creating Family Traditions

Take a moment to think back on any traditions your own family may have observed when you were growing up—especially when you were in the same age group as your child is now. Naturally, these memories will be colored by the state of your family at the time. That being said, family traditions are a way of bringing the family together, offer an element of stability and predictability to family life, and are important to cultivate whenever possible.

Most family traditions are built around such things as holidays and birthdays. The following questions are intended as food for thought:

- What traditions did your family celebrate?
- How did your family celebrate these occasions?

- Did you look forward to these traditions?
- How would you have felt of one of these traditions had been cancelled?

Whether your current family is large or is just yourself and your child, it is desirable to establish and follow family traditions. For some divorcing parents, the traditions that they had followed before the divorce were centered mostly around their ex-spouse's family. If this has happened to you, it may feel as if you have lost your family traditions. In these cases, it can be helpful to talk to friends about what special family traditions they follow in own their households, and use these ideas as a springboard for developing your own traditions. I encourage divorcing parents to create at least one *new* tradition for their post-divorce family. For example, you can celebrate a holiday you once more or less ignored, or establish a tradition of taking one weekend a year as a mini family vacation.

For instance, one divorcing mother decided to start a tradition on Halloween. She had two children, and at the time of her divorce they were four and six. Since she happened to live in a neighborhood that was conducive to trick-or-treating, in which there were a lot of young children, she decided to start a yearly Halloween tradition of inviting family, friends, and neighbors with children over to her house for pizza and soda. Once all of them had something reasonably healthy in their stomachs, the children went trick-or-treating as a group. The mother's parents volunteered to stay at her home and dole out treats while she and her children were gone. After repeating this tradition two years in a row, this mother's children eagerly looked forward to Halloween.

Chapter 16

Direction and Discipline

Socialization is one of the two primary developmental tasks of later childhood, which is roughly ages six to eleven. As was discussed in a previous chapter, socialization involves establishing relationships with peers—hopefully with two or more peer groups. However, aside from making friends, socialization also involves learning to follow the "rules of the road" that society sets forth for us. It involves developing respect for authority, including your authority as a parent. There is certainly room in the healthy socialized individual for legitimately questioning authority, and for expressing one's opinion. By the same token, a properly socialized individual has no need to flaunt or disregard authority, or to break laws out of mere whim. An unsuccessfully socialized child, in contrast, believes not just that he or she is important, but that he or she is the center of the universe and the ultimate authority.

Successfully socializing a child is a collective responsibility. It involves the school system and extended family, for example. But beyond a doubt the most important force for socialization are a child's parents.

Divorce and Socialization

One of the biggest risks to children of divorce is when parents have opposing views about what constitutes proper socialization: what are appropriate limits; how one should go about disagreeing with authority; the importance of following rules set forth for the common good; and so on. This may have been an issue in the marriage prior to the divorce, but as long as a marriage hangs together there is often a certain amount of compromising that goes on. It is hardly uncommon, for example, for one parent to think the other is either too strict or too lenient. The most typical difference is for fathers to think mothers are too lenient, while mothers believe that fathers are too strict. Usually this applies to sons even more than daughters. When I've asked fathers about this they are often willing to acknowledge it, and the rationale they offer is their belief that boys, much more so than girls, need to be kept on a "short leash," as one father put it, in order to avoid problems later on.

Researchers who observed teachers' interactions in the classroom seem to support this belief: Teachers have been observed to intervene with boys more quickly than with girls. Whether it is actually true that boys need closer monitoring than girls is not clear. But, there is no good reason to believe that girls are inherently more able and willing to follow rules than boys. What we do know is that boys are more inclined to engage in rough-and-tumble play, which may account at least in part for this bias.

Whether based in fact or fiction, in most two-parent families the parents are able to resolve any differences in how they socialize their children through an ongoing process of dialogue and compromise. In those cases where they cannot do so, the consequences quickly become evident. Children under these circumstances will play one parent off against the other. They will become manipulative and self-centered and will tend to approach any authority figure with the attitude that authority can be manipulated for personal gain.

What can happen when parents separate, of course, is that the process of parental compromise is abandoned. Worse still, what were once seen as tolerable differences in approaches can escalate into battlegrounds, with each parent actively undermining the other. In this scenario, parents move in opposite directions along the parenting continuum, with one becoming progressively stricter, the other more lenient. If this sounds at all like your situation, you are strongly urged to seek out a professional counselor to help mediate your differences and put you both on a similar path toward socializing your child. In particular, you will need this counselor to help you focus on two areas—direction and discipline—as described below.

Direction

The first of the two major parental tools for socializing children is *direction*, meaning the instructions that you give to your child, day in and day out, that are intended to steer your child on the course toward a healthy and productive adulthood. For example, you tell your child when to eat; when he or she can (and can't) have candy—and how much; when to get dressed (and what to wear); when to do homework; when to brush their teeth; when it's okay to watch television, and so on. Generally speaking, the younger the child, the more direction is needed.

Effective parents gradually encourage their children to make more decisions for themselves. An effective parent may ask an eight year old, for instance, which of two different winter coats he or she wishes to wear that day; what their child would like as a school snack; and so on. However, if it's a cold winter day in New England, the effective parent will not offer their child the option of going coatless. And the effective parent will not allow a child to ask for nothing but candy for a snack. And this brings us to the all-important issue of limit-setting.

Let there be no doubt about it: Directing children takes a lot of energy. As a divorcing parent that responsibility, which may have previously been divided (if not equally then to at least some degree), now will fall totally on your shoulders whenever your child is with you. No wonder some parents have told me that they look forward to going to work just to get a break from "policing" their children!

Direction is usually the first area in which separation has an effect. When each parent becomes a single parent, instead of a parental team, all the responsibility for providing direction falls on one person's shoulder whenever the children are with that parent. This can be tiring, if not exhausting. One father of two sons and a daughter, all younger than eight, found shared parenting to be exhausting and stressful. "I found myself yelling all the time, barking orders, saying 'no' to just about everything," he said. He solved the problem by going to the store and buying three white boards, along with erasable-ink markers. He posted all three boards on a wall in his kitchen—one for each child. Then he wrote out an after-school schedule for each child: homework time; play time; bath time; time to brush teeth; and so on. These were all linked to a timeline. His youngest son's bath came first, followed by his older son, and then his daughter. A rotating schedule for who got to choose what television program to watch was also posted. Finally, following the rules was linked to a system of small rewards. Although this father admitted that after a month there were still "occasional kinks" in the system, he was feeling a lot less stressed and there was a lot less yelling in his house when his kids were there. "To be honest," he said, "I never realized how much energy my wife was putting into just preventing chaos in the house."

Limit-Setting

Central to the task of giving children direction is limit-setting. If you think of limits as the "rules of the road," then direction becomes a process of making sure that your child lives by those rules. When parents get into conflict with one another it is most often over limits. Again, this is not unusual and in and of itself it is not necessarily a problem. Even parents whose childrearing philosophies are pretty similar may not agree on just where to set the limit in each and every area of a child's life. In two-parent families these differences are usually settled through an ongoing dialogue and a process of compromise.

In the case of parents who are divorcing, it is sometimes true that big differences in parenting philosophies—which are almost always reflected in big differences of opinion about limits—were one of the contributing factors in the ongoing marital discord. Regardless of whether this was already an issue, it is in the long-term interest of your child that both you and your ex try to establish a dialogue on this subject of limits.

When I make this suggestion to some divorcing parents, they throw up their hands in a statement of frustration. Limit-setting, they say, has always been a bone of contention, and they expect that divorce is likely to make this worse instead of better. My response to them is this: *Even a contentious dialogue about limits is better than no dialogue. Moreover, one of the worst things a parent can do for a child is to purposefully undermine the limits set by the other parent.*

If you as divorcing parents want to see to it that your child gets through these three crucial years emotionally, academically, and socially unscathed, then one of the best things you can do is to learn to compromise with each other on limits and come to some agreement on them. Here are some examples of limits that need to be agreed upon:

- Completing homework every day
- What kinds of television shows and movies (and what ratings) are permissible
- Bed times
- Cleaning up
- Chores
- Allowances

These are only a few of the more important areas in which parents who are truly interested in pursuing a child-centered divorce will be willing to compromise and cooperate in order to see to it that their children get through these three crucial years successfully. In contrast, here are some of the risks that separated parents take if one or both refuse to cooperate and compromise:

- Children who are raised with overly lax limits may be more at risk than children who are raised with what we might call overly strict limits. Of course, strictness can be overdone as well. When being strict amounts to putting a child in a behavioral straight jacket, giving them no choice at all, or not allowing them to speak their mind, it has gone too far. In that case, strictness can be as harmful to a child's development as can overly lax limits.
- Children who face inconsistent limits in a shared-parenting arrangement will become manipulative and will in time develop a low regard for authority.

Think of limits as guidelines: They tell children when they are free to act and make choices, and when they are not. For example, many children today have to bring daily snacks to school. You may purchase a variety of snacks that you consider healthy and then allow your child to decide every day which of these snacks to bring to school. This means, of course, that some snacks will not be on the list of options.

Aside from the things already mentioned, areas in which separated parents are wise to develop agreed-upon limits include:

- *Clothing*. This includes what clothes are appropriate and how much you are willing to spend on them. At some point your child may succumb to the allure of designer clothing in order to impress peers. If you decide to go in this direction at all, where will you set the limit? Is there anything wrong with buying perfectly good clothing from a consignment store? One mother, despite earning a sizable income as a physician, explained that she simply would not allow her daughter to get into the "designer clothing thing." She did not want her child to grow into an adult with such expectations. "What would happen to her if she were 30 years old and got laid off and couldn't afford her designer labels?" she asked rhetorically. "I want her to learn that you can get through life perfectly well without such things."
- *Opposite-Sex Relationships*. Many pre-teens today are tempted to put themselves into situations that they are not ready to handle.

Prime among these are experimenting with drugs—to be discussed shortly—and opposite-sex interactions. Girls as young as nine or ten, for example, may ask their parent if they can go to a movie with a boy from their class. Once again, the parent who is dealing with divorce (and a potentially contentious relationship with an ex-spouse) may be tempted to become the "good guy" by saying yes to such a request. That is a mistake. Dating needs to be placed on hold until the teen years, and is inappropriate in any form for children in the age group being discussed here. Opposite-sex interactions at this age need to be limited to public events, such as birthday parties. They should not be one-on-one experiences, and they should not be held out of direct parental supervision.

Collaborating with Teachers

Aside from your child's pediatrician, a great resource for monitoring your child's social development is his or her teacher. After letting your child's teacher know that you and your spouse have separated, it will be important to establish and maintain an open line of communication. That's not to say that you will call or e-mail your child's teacher on a daily basis. On the other hand, almost all school systems today offer parents opportunities to communicate with staff and teachers via e-mail. Before doing this, however, a brief face-to-face meeting can be very helpful.

Your child's teacher is a resource for monitoring your child's social development as well as his or her academic progress. Make sure the teacher knows to inform you if he or she observes any significant changes in your child's mood, behavior, or relationships with peers. Also, you will want to know if your child's academic progress seems to be on track, or whether some extra help may be required.

Teachers, much like pediatricians, have a chance to observe many children, and in the process they can gain a perspective on what constitutes "normal" versus what should be cause for concern. In that regard teachers can be used as sounding boards and problem-solvers. On the other hand they are not therapists, so one has to be careful not to rely so much on teachers that they will feel that they are being asked to give advice they are not qualified to offer.

Discipline

The second major parental tool for socializing children is discipline. Once again it is not unusual to find couples who are not one hundred percent in agreement when it comes to discipline, just as they are not in complete agreement when it comes to setting limits. Divorce can cause these differences to become exaggerated, as parents tend to move more toward one extreme or the other, either *over*-disciplining their child in the belief that this is the time to be more watchful and strict, or *under*-disciplining in the belief that their child is suffering enough because of the divorce and should therefore be granted some slack.

The golden rules for applying discipline to children in this age group are:

1. Tie any discipline you apply to the appropriate limits that your child's behavior has violated.
2. Always apply redirection before resorting to discipline.
3. Try as much as possible to make the punishment fit the crime.

Make no mistake about it—children aged six to eleven will definitely need discipline at times, just as they will need direction. They do not necessarily need more (or less) discipline while you are going through a divorce than they did before your split. If you allow your child to consistently violate limits, and then compound that with a failure to discipline appropriately, then you will most likely find yourself dealing with the subject matter of the next chapter—tantrums and oppositional behavior—before long.

Let's take a closer look at each of the above three guidelines for discipline.

Tie any discipline you apply to the appropriate limits that your child's behavior has violated.

If you did *not* tell your son that he couldn't eat the whole box of chocolate chip cookies you bought, then you obviously shouldn't impose discipline if he does. As obvious as this sounds, there are many times when parents seem inclined to set limits "on the fly"—in other words, as they come up. There is nothing inherently wrong with this practice, as long as discipline *follows* limit-setting.

Given how many areas of life it may be necessary to set limits and provide direction in, it is not reasonable to expect a parent to think of each and every one in advance. By the same token, it isn't really appropriate to impose discipline in an area in which there has previously been no direction. So, if the issue of how many cookies your son can eat at one time has never come up before, the thing to do the first time he eats the whole box is to establish a limit and provide him with direction. If he does this again, appropriate discipline is in order.

Divorce can create a certain amount of chaos in a parent's life. Under these circumstances it can be easy to overlook the importance of setting limits. Many a parent, angry at him- or herself, has lashed out at a child for failing to follow a limit that was never established. Rather than getting angry at themselves, these parents are better off writing off the situations as "learning experiences" and then setting clear limits for the future.

Always apply re-direction before resorting to discipline

Discipline (punishment) is something that works best when it is used sparingly. By the same token, giving children rewards for good behavior is also something that works best when it is not overdone. Therefore, before you consider disciplining your child, try redirection instead. It is best to have a rationale for any limit you establish as opposed to resorting to the old saw *"Because I said so!"* That is usually the mark of a desperate parent who has been caught without a rationale for a limit. This should not really be difficult. For example, you may impose a limit of one cookie (or candy bar, or ice cream treat) a day because you want to limit how much sugar your child takes in. This may not make sense to your child; on the other hand, it is a legitimate reason for setting a limit that has a rationale behind it. By the same reasoning, you should feel free to set limits on bedtimes; on how much television your child can watch; on how often he or she must take a bath and brush teeth; and so on. A reasonable rationale for a limit on television would be that you want your child to have a balanced lifestyle and not to devote an excessive amount of time to any one activity or interest. Similarly, you make your child brush his or her teeth to prevent tooth decay and the pain that brings.

Redirecting is pretty much self-evident: You simply point out how your child has violated a limit, instruct him or her to stop, and direct your child toward another activity. This can reduce any frustration your child may experience as a result of bumping up against a limit.

Several parents have related stories about how their children developed a habit of challenging limits by asking *"Why?"* every time one was set. Invariably, these parents found that offering to enter into a dialogue over their rationales led nowhere. Children may be children, but they quickly figure out that they may be able strike a compromise (and get more of what they want) if they can get their parent on the defensive, justifying the rationale behind a limit. There is no need to do this. Once you lay out your rationale you do not need to defend it. You are, after all, the final authority on the matter. Refusing to debate or defend your rationale is a sure way to reduce your child's efforts to challenge you.

Try as much as possible to make any punishment fit the crime

This may be the most difficult of all the ground rules for discipline for parents to apply. Your own inclinations in this area will probably be colored by how you were disciplined as a child. This may or may not be a good thing, depending on how effective your own parents were at applying this rule. Moreover, as was mentioned earlier, differences in how their parents set limits and disciplined their children often turn out to lie at the root of much marital discord. Sadly, it is something that couples often choose to overlook when they are courting. Perhaps they minimize its importance because they believe their own marriage will be different from their parents'. More likely, they just don't realize how much these differences can come back to haunt them later on. As you work your way through your divorce and eventually contemplate finding a new relationship, you would be wise to learn more about how any potential partner was raised. How did this individual's parents set limits? How did they discipline? Are these consistent with your own ideas about limits and discipline?

The important thing to keep in mind is that children aged six to eleven experience *any* deprivation as very painful. They are still at an age at which, from their perspective, the world pretty much revolves around them. From their vantage point, their own perceived needs take priority. Therefore, to be denied hurts.

This means that it is not necessary to impose severe discipline in order for it to be keenly felt by your child. The boy who eats a whole box of cookies a second time will feel the pain of being denied access to any cookies the next day. In other words, it is not necessary to take away cookies for a month as discipline for breaking the established limit.

Whatever discipline you decide to impose, it is important not to merely threaten it, but to follow through and impose it. Children learn remarkably quickly when a parent is "all talk and no action." Indeed, no one is more pathetic than the parent who repeatedly threatens, *"No dessert for you tonight!"* and then gives a child dessert. As their child quickly learns to ignore these empty threats, the parent becomes increasingly exasperated, often to the point of screaming. That screaming is a sure sign of a parent who has failed to follow through with the three-step process of setting a limit, redirecting, and then appropriately disciplining their child.

There continues to be debate around the issue of corporal punishment, with some parents and experts taking the position that there is nothing wrong with the occasional slap on the behind. Many states have gone so far as to pass legislation affirming parents' right to employ at least moderate physical punishment. This has a long tradition in America, stemming from the eighteenth-century admonition: *"Spare the rod and spoil the child!"* That advice notwithstanding, research suggests that parents who conscientiously work to apply the ground rules presented in this chapter should rarely if ever need to resort to corporal punishment to discipline their children. If you do, the final rule is this: *The less often you resort to it, the more effective corporal punishment will be.* In other words, the six year old who gets a slap on the behind once or twice a year will be more likely to comply with limits than the boy who receives that punishment once or twice a week.

* * *

As you and your ex work your way through the process of your divorce, keep in mind that, the more similar you are in how you each approach these critical parental responsibilities, the more likely your child will emerge from these three crucial years in good shape, academically, emotionally, and socially. You do not have to agree completely on these issues. However, if you are unable to strike a reasonable compromise in this area, it would be in the long-term interest of your child for you and your ex to seek professional counseling in order to find common ground. Otherwise, your child's behavior will probably begin to reflect this sooner than later. Telltale symptoms can include declining school performance, problems getting along with teachers or peers, and aggressive or defiant behavior.

Chapter 17

Tantrums and Oppositional Behavior

The occasional temper tantrum, meltdown, and even oppositional behavior (defiance) in children ages six to eleven may be as inevitable as death and taxes. In and of themselves, these behaviors should not be a cause for concern. In fact, they should be expected if you are doing your job as a parent and encouraging your child to gradually develop his or her independence. There are bound to be occasions when you and your child will butt heads over limits, or when what you want your child to do is not what he or she wants to do. This will be true whether or not you are going through a divorce. However, the stress of separation and divorce does place an added strain on young children's ability to cope, and one potential result of that strain—an increase in tantrums and oppositional behavior—is the topic of this chapter.

Amanda

Amanda, age ten, was described by both her parents as a model child. A high achiever in school, she was also active in drama, gymnastics, and horseback riding. In contrast, her thirteen-year-old brother, Nick, had been an underachiever in school for several years. He complained that school was boring and used that as an excuse for blowing off homework assignments. The result was a bright teen with poor grades.

Amanda already knew that she wanted to go to college and had thought about two possible careers: a teacher or a veterinarian. Her teachers found her a joy, and one of them described Amanda as "the hardest working student in my class." All of that changed rather suddenly when Amanda's parents informed her of their decision to separate.

There had been conflict in this marriage for several years and later, in counseling, it became apparent that there was a link between this parental discord and tension and both Nick's underachievement and what one could almost describe as Amanda's "overachievement." Although both parents clearly loved both of their children, any true affection between the couple had long since withered and died. The result was a materially comfortable but emotionally cold household. The family occasionally did things together, but when they did Nick participated reluctantly and interacted with others minimally. Amanda, on the other hand, played the role of entertainer, talking about her activities and social life so as to loosen up the mood.

Within a month of her parents' separation, Amanda "transformed" (in her mother's words) and went from being the perfect child to "the child from hell." She became incredibly moody. As her mother put it: "All of a sudden I've gone from a great mom to a mother who can't do anything right, whose opinion on just about everything is wrong, and who is bent on persecuting my daughter. No matter what I say she responds by either rolling her eyes, getting mad, or bursting into tears."

Amanda became very oppositional and critical of her mother at this time. Her father, while spared the brunt of his daughter's wrath, nevertheless noticed moodiness. And when Amanda was with him in the condo he'd rented he noticed that she was inclined to push the limits much more than she ever had. She insisted, for instance, on being able to watch "R"-rated movies with friends, even though the long-established rule in the family was that neither child could watch such movies until they were 16 years old. He also noticed that she'd begun using make-up and wanted to buy clothes that struck him as a bit too sexy for her age.

Amanda's behavior was speaking for her. Her oppositional behavior expressed her "opposition" to her parents' decision to separate. Although she'd never been consciously aware of it, her efforts to be a perfect child were intended, in part, to be a way of keeping her family together. On some level both Amanda and Nick were aware of their parents' unhappiness. Whereas Nick's behavior reflected hopelessness about it, Amanda's represented an attempt to fix things.

Tantrums, Defiance, and Divorce

Child development can be thought of as a process of gradual independence. That being the case, it would be unreasonable to expect psychologically healthy children never to oppose their parents. In fact, parents who attempt to totally quash any such behavior are doing their children a distinct disfavor. At the same time, as the example of Amanda shows, the sudden emergence of frequent and intense temper tantrums and/or oppositional behavior in a child who has not previously displayed such behaviors (or at least not frequently or intensely) may be a sign of anxiety and insecurity that has its roots in the stress of separation and divorce.

The best way for the separated parent to approach such behavior is to begin by taking a moment to reflect on the context. Is this behavior familiar, or is it relatively new? Is it behavior that is more or less consistent with your child's personality, or does it seem like he or she has suddenly become a different person? If it is new, and if it seems to be a reaction to your separation, then here are some guidelines to keep in mind when dealing with it:

"Translate" behavior into words

Again, keep in mind that children often "speak" through their actions as much or more so than they do through their words. This being the case, it can be helpful for you to open a dialogue about your separation. That isn't to say that you should try to justify your decision to your child, or even go into detail about your marital problems and travails. That approach almost invariably will put you on the defensive and trying to place the blame on your spouse. Rather, this dialogue should be about how your *child* feels about your separation, and how it has affected *his* or *her* life.

The oppositional behavior you are seeing may well be an expression of anxiety and/or anger about your divorce. After all, your child is also going through this major upheaval—and he or she didn't choose it. In opening this dialogue you are in effect offering to put your child's actions into words. When doing so it is important not to pressure your child to speak his or her mind about your divorce, but rather to let your child know this is an acceptable topic of conversation. Moreover, it is important to let children know that they are entitled to have feelings about the divorce, including sadness, anger, and anxiety.

The best time to initiate this dialogue is *not* when your child is in the midst of a tantrum, or when you find yourself going to toe-to-toe over some limit that he or she has violated. Rather, the best time is when your child is relatively calm and not distracted, and when you find that you have a few uninterrupted moments together. You can break the ice by bringing up the subject in a general way, such as *"How are you feeling about the divorce?"* Wait to see what kind of reaction you get. Don't be surprised if you get a minimal response, such as a shrug of the shoulders or a few weakly muttered and unintelligible words. This is often a child's initial reaction, for two reasons: They may not be able to find the right words to express how they feel, and they may be uncertain as to how you will react.

Follow up on any icebreaker by suggesting that you can handle whatever it is your child has to say, and whatever feelings they may express. One mother put it this way to her two children: "I know you don't want to hurt my feelings, but I also know you probably have some feelings at times about what's going on. I just want you both to know that I'm an adult, and that I love you both very much, and I can handle anything you have to say. It won't change our relationships one bit.

A divorcing father recounted the following conversation with his eight-year-old son: "You know, it's okay with me if you ever have something you'd like to ask or say about me and Mom getting a divorce. You might have some questions, and you might have some feelings. You could be sad, for example, or scared, or mad. It would be okay for us to talk about that."

You should not expect your child to immediately begin speaking openly about how she or he is feeling about your divorce and how it is affecting his or her life. However, if you restate your openness to such a dialogue once in a while, you may eventually get a response. Hopefully, the words your child uses to express his or her feelings will gradually replace the behavior that had previously been "speaking for your child.

Of course, you may not have a solution that will completely satisfy your child. The solution that most children seek is to not have their parents divorce at all. Obviously, this is one wish that you can't grant. Similarly, if you have had to relocate, or if your standard of living has declined somewhat as a result of a change in finances, you may not be in a position to reverse those changes either. On the other hand, some of your child's anxiety may come from fear of the unknown: *"What will happen next?"* Being able to talk about that can go a long way toward reducing any insecurity your child may be experiencing.

Consider limited compromises

Not all issues are truly worthy of going to the barricades. Offering limited compromises is not the same as abandoning your limits and expectations for your child. In an earlier chapter you were warned against the dangers of failing to stick to the reasonable limits you set, and failing to follow through on any discipline you mete out in response to misbehavior. Both of those tendencies—which may happen more often under the stress of divorce—will lead only to more oppositional behavior that challenges your authority and to tantrums in response to frustration. That said, it is equally true that parents need not be overly rigid. They key to effective parenting lies in learning how to manage the delicate balance between setting limits (and being in control) versus compromising (and allowing your child to have his or her voice). This is especially true at a time of family upheaval such as separation. A lot depends, of course, on just how many how many rules and limits you establish. A wise parent will limit these to those that are most essential—things like eating meals, bedtimes, school responsibilities, what constitutes appropriate attire, what television shows or movies can and can't be watched, and so on. On such matters there may be relatively little room for compromise, as you feel that compromising would not be good for your child. In that case oppositional behavior must be met head-on, even if it leads to anger or tears.

In many other areas, however, it may be possible to be open to negotiation and compromise. This teaches your child to be persistent and to be clear about why he or she wants something or wants to do something. In every case, though, *you* need to be the one to approve a compromise.

As an example, consider the issue of clothing. As your child gets to be eight, nine, and ten years old she or he may very well begin to express some opinions in this area. No doubt this will be influenced by what peers are wearing. You should have some standards (and your child should be aware of them) about what constituters *unacceptable* attire. That limit being set, this still leaves a lot of room for what would be acceptable. When you take your child shopping for clothes, you should first establish—in advance—a budget. This budget should be firm, with very little wiggle room. If your child insists on buying name-brand clothing, then she or he may have to settle for a lot fewer clothes. Moreover, whatever he or she chooses must still not violate your limits of what's acceptable. This approach will probably not be conflict-free. However, it allows your child to develop some sense of empowerment, within limits.

This, in turn, helps develop healthy self-esteem and teaches your child that it is possible to be an individual while still complying with rules.

When they separate, both parents should expect this issue to raise its head again. When this happens their responses are critical. If they decide to make up new rules and limits that differ from one another, they can expect an ongoing process of limit-testing in which the stricter parent will become the bad guy. That does the child no good; moreover, eventually both parents will encounter oppositional and limit-testing behavior as their child gradually loses respect for any limits that are set. In this case the parents' differing dress standards provide fertile ground for a child to act out his or her anger about the separation.

A child-centered approach to divorce would require separating parents to have a private dialogue about issues such as clothing, and then to present a common front. This may not eliminate limit-testing, but it will definitely curtail any tendency for the child to become manipulative.

Summing Up

An increase in limit-testing as well as temper tantrums—sometimes in children who have never shown such behavior before—should come as no surprise to the newly separated parent. Chances are your child is speaking to you through his or her behavior. Your child is expressing opposition to your decision to separate; however, your child cannot influence your decision. But, you can open a dialogue that allows your child to verbalize his or her thoughts and feelings. That, along with an effort to cooperate and set common limits, can go a long way toward ameliorating this problem.

Chapter 18

School and Social Phobias

A child's insecurity in the face of parental separation will manifest itself in sudden changes of behavior. We've already addressed changes such as increases in tantrums and "oppositional behavior." Other changes that are symptomatic of anxiety and insecurity that can crop up during a divorce include a sudden fear of going to school, a sudden unwillingness to socialize, even with well-known peers and friends, and/or a sudden refusal to participate in activities that a child previously enjoyed.

School phobia can emerge during a divorce, but it can also be a response to other significant changes in the family structure that create insecurity and anxiety. For example, children can develop school phobia when a parent who previously was home every night gets a new job that requires him or her to be away from home overnight several times a month. This disruption in the fabric of family life can be enough to trigger some insecurity in a child.

The emergence of a phobia is another case of behavior speaking for the child. Oppositional behavior bespeaks anger; phobias bespeak anxiety.

Understanding and Overcoming School Phobia

All phobias have one thing in common: They start out as small issues that grow until they take on a life of their own—one that eventually takes over a person's life. They also typically emerge at a time of upheaval and stress. This is as true for children as it is for adults. Consider, as an example, test-taking anxiety. Many people report feeling some anxiety at the prospect of taking a test. Few people, however, go on to experience a full-blown "test phobia." Typically, the factor that makes the critical difference is whether that person's life is generally in order or whether it is in a state of crisis and upheaval. Stability usually means that the anxiety will soon fade; in contrast, chronic stress can facilitate the emergence of a phobia, as the following case illustrates.

Aiden

Aiden's parents described him as a boy who had always had a tendency to worry. The youngest of three sons, he had a track record of missing school due to illness about twice that of his brothers. Often these "illnesses" involved stomach pain and nausea, and occasionally vomiting. Aiden's parents had long suspected that anxiety was the real culprit behind these periodic aches and pains, not germs or viruses. However, they were never able to pin down the factors that triggered them, though they suspected that they had something to do with school. Aiden was a shy boy who had few friends. He disliked being the focus of attention, and whenever he was facing an upcoming school event that might put him there he would get "sick." That had happened twice, for example, when his class was scheduled to put on their annual spring concert. So long as Aiden's "illnesses" were not too frequent, his parents were willing to tolerate them.

This situation changed radically soon after Aiden's parents told the boys that they were separating. Aiden's father, they learned, had accepted a job in a city that was three hours away. It had not originally been his intention to change jobs or move; rather, economic realities had forced him to do so. He would, the boys were told, be returning every weekend and would be hosting the boys at Aiden's grandparents' home, which had enough room for them.

Within a week of learning this—in fact, the day after his father first drove off to his new job—Aiden came down with the worst stomachache he'd ever had. It happened shortly after he got to school, and he was sent to see the school nurse. When he got to the nurse's office he vomited, which triggered a phone call to Aiden's mother to come get him.

Aiden's mother worked part-time, but this was one of the days she worked, so it was rather inconvenient for her to have to leave to go fetch

Aiden. With her husband out of town until Friday night, though, she had no alternative.

The next morning Aiden awoke with another stomachache. He cried and told his mother he did not want to go to school. The reason? He was afraid he would vomit in his classroom, which he would find humiliating. "I'm going to throw up," he told his mother, "and the other kids will make fun of me." For a child with Aiden's shyness this was indeed a dreadful proposition.

Thus began Aiden's school phobia. It may have had its roots in his shyness and sensitivity, but clearly it was his parents' separation and his father's absence that led to the full-blown phobia. He was expressing his anxiety in this way, albeit unconsciously. What was he afraid of? Two things: First, he had always looked to his father as a source of comfort, even more so than his mother. Also, his father's plans seemed vague, and Aiden did not know what would lie ahead for him and his brothers.

Overcoming Phobias

Some people appear to be susceptible to phobias, perhaps because their nervous system is simply "wired" that way. That was probably true for Aiden, who had always been a bit "nervous." The stress of his parents' separation was sufficient to push him over the line, however, from simple nervousness to full-blown phobia.

Aiden's parents sought the advice of their pediatrician, who then referred them to a therapist who specialized in working with children, and in particular children of divorce. What follows is a summary of the process that they were guided through in order to deal with Aiden's phobia:

- *Open the dialogue*
  This is the same advice offered earlier with respect to oppositional behavior and tantrums. In this case it was the therapist who put Aiden's behavior into words. "You are upset about your parents' separation," she offered, "and you probably don't like it that you won't be seeing your father during the week." Initially Aiden opened up about his feelings only to the therapist, but in time he was able to express his anxiety and ask questions to his parents. This brought them into the light of day—rather than being locked up inside Aiden—where they could be addressed. One solution

was that Aiden's father purchased a video camera for his laptop computer so that father and son could have a face-to-face conversation via computer every night.

- *Work with school personnel*
  It may not be necessary to inform your child's teacher the first time he or she expresses anxiety about going to school (or, as in Aiden's case, the first time your child misses school because of some phantom illness); however, if this begins to happen on a regular basis (say two or three times a month), then a heads-up to the teacher is a good idea.

  Chances are your child's teacher has encountered phobic behavior before, and has some ideas about what to do. Also, schools have resources such school psychologists who can be consulted. Sometimes an intervention as simple as a teacher making a little extra effort to greet a child on arrival to the classroom can make a big difference when it comes to reducing anxiety. Coming into a welcoming, warm, and secure environment can help allay a lot of anxiety. It makes a child feel special. This, in addition to being able to talk about his concerns and having increased contact with his father, helped Aiden a lot.

- *Express confidence in the future*
  As a rule, anxiety begets anxiety. Many parents are unaware that their child's anxiety actually reflects their own. In other words, the more anxious you are about your own divorce and what lies ahead for you, the more anxious your child is apt to be. If your child happens to be one of the millions of people who are born emotionally sensitive, there is a good chance that his or her anxiety will show up in some physical manifestation such as the frequent stomachaches just mentioned, headaches, or in some other form, such as school phobia. Therefore, it is important, regardless of how you feel privately, that outwardly you consistently express confidence about the future. Your motto through these three crucial years should be: *"We are a family and we are going to be just fine."* If you need to seek out a counselor to use as a sounding board for your personal anxieties; fine. Or, you can turn to friends or family for support and encouragement. Whatever you do, try your best to communicate optimism to your child.

- *Increase comforting rituals*
  Parent–child and other family rituals have already been discussed. Incorporating such rituals into family life on a regular, even a

daily, basis increases children's sense of security and well-being. If you find that such rituals have slipped out of your life, try putting them back in place. In addition to reinstituting rituals that may have fallen by the wayside, you can institute new rituals. Examples of such rituals that parents have shared with me include a daily "family reading time." In this ritual, parent and child visit the library and select several books to read. Then, every night, they sit together and the parent reads a chapter or two aloud. Other rituals include watching a particular television show together, and having after-dinner dessert together.

- *Provide support to "desensitize" the phobia*
Psychologists have long made use of a technique called *desensitization* to help people overcome phobias. Despite its formidable name, desensitization is actually a simple process. Basically, to desensitize anxiety you need to do two things: have a person *relax*, and then *gradually* expose them to the things that makes them anxious. As applied to school phobia, what you want to do is try to see to it that your child is as calm as possible before having to go to school, and then ease him or her through the process of getting to school. This means, for example, making morning before school time comfortable. Make sure your child eats a nutritious but tasty breakfast. Put on some children's music, or a morning children's television show, while your child eats and gets dressed. If necessary, get up 15 to 20 minutes earlier in order to make time for these comforting additions to your routine. Then, when it is time to go to school, make it as easy as possible. If your child takes a bus, accompany him or her to the bus stop and wait for the bus. All the while, keep up a friendly dialogue. Tell your child what he or she will be doing at school that day, especially things you know he or she looks forward to: "*Today is a gym day*"; "*Today you have art class*," and so on. Remind your child that his friends will be glad to see him. If your child balks at getting on the school bus, avoid a head-to-head confrontation. Instead, offer to drive him or her to school, say, once or twice a week. Offer to do this for three to four weeks.

Seeking Professional Help

Usually, if you follow the above guidelines for three to four weeks, a school phobia will have subsided. Don't be overly concerned if it pops up now and again, as that is normal for phobias. If there is a morning when your child expresses anxiety about going to school, just repeat one or more of the above steps. On the other hand, if you do find the school phobia getting worse instead of better after a month or so of following these guidelines, you might consider consulting with a therapist, as Aiden's parents did. Be sure to seek help from a therapist who specializes in working with children in your child's age group. This person may also want to contact school personnel and will need your written permission to do so. Chances are this therapist will coach you and your child through a desensitization program of some kind. One thing to avoid, however, is any kind of "behavior modification" program that seeks to give your child some kind of reward for going to school. This can set up a bad precedent for the future, as your child may come to expect to be rewarded for doing things that should be normal responsibilities, like brushing teeth or getting dressed.

Chapter 19

Guarding against Academic Failure

Reading is a critical academic skill that can suffer if a child is experiencing excessive anxiety or is distracted. Divorce represents the kind of upheaval in a child's life that can easily create exactly such anxiety or distractibility. Research has shown that children who fall behind academically during the three crucial years of parental separation and divorce have a hard time catching up and may be in for a longstanding academic struggle. For children who are between the ages of six and eleven, therefore, divorcing parents need to be vigilant for early signs of academic trouble, especially in the area of reading, but also in the areas of basic math and writing skills. Then, if they detect a problem in the making, they need to know how to intervene.

Team Up with Your Child's Teachers

We have touched on this issue already but it is so important that it is worth repeating: Your child's teachers, like your child's pediatrician, can be an important ally to you over the next three years. However, neither can be as effective an ally as they may want to be if they are either unaware of your circumstances or have to guess at it.

- *What to say, what not to say.*
  You need to make your child's teacher aware of the essentials: that you are going through a divorce; what your child's living and visiting arrangements are; and who else besides yourself is authorized

to pick up your child from school. You need *not* discuss the reasons for your divorce, which are better kept to yourself.

- *Be vigilant for changes.*

While you do not need to communicate much with teachers about the details of your divorce, you *should* share any observations you make regarding changes in your child's behavior or overall emotional state. Be on the lookout in particular for increases in moodiness (such as more frequent meltdowns or tantrums), loss of interest in things your child previously enjoyed very much, and distractibility. These may or may not carry over into the classroom. For example, just because your eight year old becomes more testy and moody at home does not necessarily mean that he or she will act that way in school. Some children limit their "acting out" over a divorce to home. Or, they limit it to their relationship with only one parent (typically the one they feel most secure with). However, it is possible that changes you see at home do carry over into the classroom, where they may interfere with learning or cause social problems. That's why you want the communication with your child's teacher to be a two-way street. Not only should you communicate any significant changes you may notice, but you want your child's teacher to do the same. This will provide you with an opportunity to coordinate efforts with school personnel and develop a plan that will nip any potential problems in the bud, as the following example shows.

Megan's father had moved out of the house the summer before she started fourth grade. Her parents had decided to wait to tell their two children about their decision to divorce until the school year was over, thinking that this would give them more than two months to adjust to the idea.

Megan and her brother slept over at their father's apartment one evening during the week and every other weekend. While her brother seemed fine with this, Megan missed her father when she wasn't with him. The result was that when she was with her mother she tended to isolate herself in her room, where she would lie on her bed and read or draw.

Megan's mother noticed this change, but whenever she asked if Megan was okay the girl would say yes. Because she had always volunteered in her children's classrooms, Megan's mother had good relationships with their teachers. She shared her observation with Megan's teacher. "I'm glad you told me that," the teacher replied, "because the one thing I've noticed is that Megan seems to be distracted or daydreaming quite a bit in class. If I call on her half the time it's obvious that she hasn't been paying attention."

Megan's distractibility, if it was not addressed promptly, could easily cause her to fall behind academically. And if she fell behind in fourth grade, she could well be playing catch-up for years to come.

With Megan's parents' approval, the teacher arranged for Megan to meet weekly with the school social worker. In that setting Megan was able to share her feelings about her parents' separation and how much she missed her father. She loved both her parents, and truly believed that they both loved her, and she hadn't wanted to upset them by telling them how she felt.

The school social worker, of course, could not change the reality of Megan's parents' divorce. However, after a couple of months of meetings—and talking about her feelings—Megan's teacher noticed that the girl was now paying attention again in class. And Megan's mother noticed that she had stopped spending as much time alone in her room.

- *Look for signs of regression.*

"Regression" may sound like another complicated psychological term, but its meaning is simple: Children regress when they start acting in a way or ways that they did when they were younger. An example of regression that we've already discussed is bedwetting in a child who has been potty trained for some time. The following case illustrates another example of regression.

Emma

Emma had always been a somewhat shy child. When she was in day care, for example, the children would practice each year for a spring concert in which the group would sing together for their parents. Emma's day-care teachers described her as having one of the best and loudest voices through all of these practice sessions. On the day of the concert, however, Emma was visibly nervous and had to go to the bathroom multiple times. When it came time for her to sing with the rest of the chorus she stood there and cried instead. This happened two years in a row.

Over time, Emma seemed to overcome her social anxiety. By the time she was in fifth grade she again participated in a class concert, and this time she sang and smiled all the way through it. Then her parents filed for divorce and Emma found herself living a complicated life in which she rotated between the house her mother stayed in and an apartment that her father was renting until the divorce was finalized.

Emma had always been a compliant girl, eager to help and not one to complain. Like Megan, Emma knew her parents both loved her; still, she did not like having to pack her school work, clothes, and favorite stuffed animals into two backpacks and follow a complex schedule that she'd had no say in creating. In addition, no matter which parent's home she was in, she found that she missed the other one terribly. And like Megan, she didn't really feel free to express these feelings to her parents, whom she perceived as wanting to hear that everything was okay.

Then Emma's parents and teachers noticed a change. Specifically, Emma seemed to be regressing into her former self. The first sign of trouble was when she told her parents that she wanted to drop out of the school chorus, as well as a children's drama program that she'd been enrolled in for three years, which she enjoyed and that had seemed to help her come out of her shell. In addition, whereas she had become a student who never hesitated to raise her hand to contribute in class, she abruptly stopped doing so. And when she was invited to a sleepover birthday party by her best friend, she opted out. Finally, her parents began receiving e-mails from Emma's teacher alerting them to the fact that she was not completing all of her homework and that her grades were falling.

Emma's previous gains over her innate shyness, her overall social development, as well as her academic progress, were now all at risk. Fortunately, because they were vigilant, and because they were willing to cooperate in their daughter's interest, Emma's parents were able to intervene. Following a conference with school personnel, they arranged for her to meet weekly with a female child therapist, with whom Emma opened up. Within a month the therapist was including Emma's parents in some of the sessions, which covered a lot of ground, including how Emma felt about her rotating schedule, her sadness when she was not with both of her parents, and some lingering doubts she was harboring about whether she was as "smart" as some of her friends. As it turned out, the last of these had its roots in Emma's shyness as a toddler, which she'd perceived at the time as a personal failure.

Emma's story had a happy ending. In time she was able to recover her self-confidence and get back into the mainstream of social activities and development. Although they still went ahead with their divorce, her parents came to an accommodation about Emma's schedule that made it less disjointed, and at the end of the school year they both attended a performance put on by her drama class.

Monitoring Student Performance

Emma's experience underlines how important it is to monitor children's school performance as well as their behavior through these three crucial years. A drop-off in school performance, and/or a change in behavior, are often the first sign of trouble, and early intervention can save you and your child a lot of heartache later on.

All schools will offer parents opportunities for periodic parent–teacher conferences. As useful as these are, for a parent going through a divorce they are not sufficient to allow for the close monitoring you need to do. During the three crucial years you need to have much more regular communication with teachers. In effect, you need an open line of communication so that you can monitor your child's progress in the critical areas of reading and math, as well as his or her social progress in making friends, participating, and following rules.

Some school systems today also offer parents the opportunity to communicate with teachers directly via e-mail. In the years ahead, more and more school districts will undoubtedly do the same. It is important to establish this communication immediately after first meetings your child's teacher, which is usually through a meet-and-greet session prior to the school year. If you are already midway into the school year, ask to have a brief meeting with the teacher to break the news about the divorce and establish the fact that you are interested in closely monitoring your child's academic progress. Make sure the teacher knows you want to know as soon as possible if your child appears to be falling behind academically, especially with respect to reading and math, and that you also would like the teacher to give you a heads-up about any behavioral problems in the classroom.

For children in early grades (first to third), some teachers employ a technique for monitoring students' behavior on a daily basis. These vary in outward form but they all work the same way. Typically a child is given a sheet of paper at the beginning of each school week. This sheet of paper will come home every night, along with that days' homework, in a folder. One teacher, for example, used a sheet with a drawing of five bones on it—one for each school day. Each day this teacher would color in the bone for that day for each child. A green bone meant an excellent day in terms of classroom behavior. A yellow bone some minor behavioral issues. Finally, a red bone indicated poor day, behaviorally speaking. At the outset of the school year this teacher asked parents to check out their child's "bone" every day and comment on it to their child. Children who got at least four green bones and no red bones in a week could choose a decorative sticker to put on their folder. In contrast, a red bone would trigger an e-mail from the teacher describing the behavior that led to that bone and just how concerned the teacher was about it. One parent, for instance, received an e-mail explaining that her son's class was a bit out of control because the cold weather had precluded outside recess four days in a row. As a result, the teacher wrote, many of the boys in the class were getting antsy, and as a result several that day had gone home with red bones. Another parent received an e-mail explaining that her son was acting increasingly aggressively toward others and had to be placed in time-out twice that day.

Systems like the above "bone technique" may be implemented by your child's teachers, and are a useful way of monitoring a child's behavior at school. They are a useful heads-up for when you need to look a bit more closely at what may be going on. If your child's teacher does not use such a technique, you might suggest it, at least for a while. You can be the one to administer any rewards, at home.

Supervise Homework

As a divorcing parent you must appreciate how critical your child's literacy is to his or her future welfare. In the critical areas—reading, spelling, and basic math—your child cannot be allowed to lag, at least not without getting any additional help he or she may need.

The advent of the No Child Left Behind legislation in 2001 brought with it many more demands on children to learn basic skills and to do so quickly. Children now begin bringing home homework in kindergarten, and it never ends. Their homework may not require hours of work, but it will be important, because teachers' lesson plans generally assume that the children in their class have completed the assigned homework from the night before. For the youngest children this will include basic letter and number recognition. From there it will advance to basic reading and basic math skills.

Teaching techniques are always changing, and so you should not expect your child's homework to look anything like the homework you may remember doing at their age. Supervising their homework may therefore mean that you will first have to read the instructions to parents that often accompany homework in order to understand how it needs to be done.

As time consuming as it may be, monitoring your child's homework to make sure it has been done and done correctly may be the most important investment of time you as a parent can make during this developmental stage. Literacy paves the way for all that follows, including social development, psychological health, and economic success.

Read with Your Child

Along with taking the time to monitor homework, reading together is an easy and effective way to monitor academic progress. All libraries today have substantial sections devoted to children's books. Ask your child's teacher what level books you should be looking at. Then let your child pick a few from that group that strike him or her as interesting. Next, set aside twenty minutes a day for your child to read to you. As long as the stories are interesting to your child this will never be a chore.

You do not have to become an expert in reading—your child's teacher has that responsibility. However, the parent who has already been in the habit of reading with their child *before* separating has the advantage of having a "baseline," meaning that they have a good sense of where their child has difficulty and how well he is progressing in reading more complex material.

What you want to be alert for are the things mentioned at the outset of this chapter, namely anxiety that leads to distractibility and difficulty concentrating. A child's anxiety over separation can very easily manifest itself in sudden difficulties reading, and not anything the child might say.

If you notice any particular areas of difficulty that your child encounters regularly, or if you notice a sudden drop-off in the ease with which he or she is able to read, have a talk with your child's teacher as soon as possible. Ask if the teacher has also noticed any changes. It may turn out to be nothing to be concerned about. And if it does appear to be an issue, you and the teacher will be in a position to intervene early.

Summing Up

The effects that parental separation and divorce can have on a child's academic progress are as important as any discussed in this book. Monitoring your child's progress, staying in touch with teachers, and working together to correct any academic problems early is one key to seeing your child safely through the three crucial years.

Chapter 20

Alcohol and Drugs

S ome parents act surprised when, in talking about children ages six to eleven, I start talking about alcohol, drugs, and sex. My response is always the same: Don't be naïve, and don't be surprised. Consider the following facts that have been established by surveys of children and teens:

- The age at which children first experiment with alcohol or drugs has declined steadily over the past 25 years. Today, the pre-teen years are the starting point for the first use of cigarettes, alcohol, and prescription drugs.
- Nicotine serves as a "gateway drug" for the use of alcohol and other drugs. In other words, children who smoke are much more likely to drink and experiment with drugs.
- The greatest increases in drug use among children and teens involve the use of prescription drugs such as tranquilizers and painkillers.
- The majority of teens who enter drug rehabilitation programs report starting their drug use prior to age thirteen.
- A *lack of parental supervision* is associated with greater risk for alcohol and drug use.
- Drugs are readily available in virtually every American high school, and increasingly in our intermediate schools.
- Simplistic approaches such as putting up signs on schools that say "Drug-Free School Zone" do little or nothing to prevent drug use.
- Early drug and alcohol use is associated with early sexual activity.

Of all of the above, the one fact that separating parents need to keep in mind is this: *parental separation is often associated with a decrease in child supervision.*

Given this, plus the other facts cited above, it makes sense that sex and drugs are not topics that should be put on hold until your child reaches adolescence. A parent–child dialogue about both can and should start by age seven.

Alcohol, Society, and Divorce

Some cultures introduce children to alcohol through rituals and traditions. The purpose of these rituals appears to be a means of including them in, and thereby bonding them to, the larger family. In these cases the amount of liquor that the child is allowed to consume is almost always very little, and is not likely to cause a problem.

In contrast, consider the fact that high school-age teens will engage in drinking rituals that involve sitting in a chair, having a funnel placed in their mouths, and then having beer after beer poured into the funnel. If you want your child to become one of these teens, then *don't* begin talking about alcohol and drugs until they are teenagers. However, if your goal is to prevent your child from deciding that such a ritual is a good idea, you need to start talking about drugs and alcohol now.

Americans consume enormous amounts of alcohol. It is a legal drug. Alcohol abuse is directly correlated with increased risk of cancer and cardiovascular disease, but people continue to use alcohol to help them relax, to unwind, or to cope with anxiety and stress. Although children *begin* using alcohol (and drugs) in a social context (because their friends are doing it) and for experimental reasons (to see how it feels), they are just as vulnerable as adults to using them to relieve stress or anxiety. And it should be very clear to the reader by now that separation and divorce create stress and anxiety. Add to that the fact that separated parents may find themselves stretched for time to supervise their children, and it's easy to see how substance abuse can become a problem at an early age. Parents are typically shocked, in fact, when they later learn just how young their children were when they started drinking or using drugs. You don't want to be one of those parents.

Drug Education

Drug education is just that: It is educating your child on the effects that alcohol and drugs have on people. You as a parent are in the best position to provide that education. It should start before your child is tempted to experiment, meaning it should begin by age seven at the very latest. Books are available at local libraries that can be used for this purpose. Written at a child's reading level, you can read and discuss them with your child. If that is not convenient, what follows is some basic information that you should share with your child. It is written here at a level that children can generally understand:

- *Cigarettes*
  Cigarettes contain *nicotine.* Smoking a cigarette will cause your heart to beat faster. It will also make you feel dizzy. Cigarette smoke contains *tar,* a sticky black substance that coats your lungs and makes your body less able to get oxygen. Our bodies need oxygen, which we get through our lungs. Without enough oxygen we will die. People who smoke cigarettes for many years can have so much difficulty getting enough oxygen into their body through their lungs that they have to carry oxygen tanks and wear masks on their faces to help them breathe.
- *Alcohol*
  Beer, wine, and whiskey all contain *alcohol.* When a person drinks alcohol, their heart slows down and their muscles move more slowly. A little alcohol makes a person feel relaxed. But a lot of alcohol makes a person sleepy. A lot of alcohol can also make a person so dizzy that they fall down and get hurt. It is possible to drink so much alcohol that your heart will stop and you will die. Bad people sometimes try to get children to drink alcohol so that the child will fall asleep and the bad person can then hurt or steal that child.
- *Marijuana*
  Marijuana is a plant that contains a chemical that is a *hallucinogen.* When someone smokes marijuana in a cigarette it can make them feel relaxed. But it can also cause them to see things that aren't there. Sometimes people mix other drugs into marijuana that causes them to have really bad nightmares that they believe are really happening. People who smoke marijuana often lose interest in things that they once liked to do. They become lazy, and they usually start doing badly in school. The smoke from marijuana cigarettes contains the same *tar* as regular cigarettes, which damages your lungs.
- *Cocaine*
  Cocaine is a *stimulant,* meaning that it makes your heart beat really fast. You can either smoke cocaine or sniff it through your nose.

Cocaine can make you feel excited or happy. But people some-times die after using cocaine because their hearts beat too fast or else start beating in the wrong way. People who try to sell you cocaine, or even offer to give you some for free, can also put bad chemicals in it that can make you have terrible nightmares that you think are really happening.

- *Sleeping Pills*
  Sleeping pills are *tranquilizers,* meaning that they help people go to sleep. They are sometimes used by adults who are having a hard time sleeping. But if a person uses tranquilizers for a long time it can be very hard for them to stop using them, even if they want to. Tranquilizers can be dangerous because they slow down your heart rate. If someone takes too many tranquilizers, or if they drink alcohol with tranquilizers, their heart can stop and they will die.
- *Painkillers*
  Sometimes adults who have had a bad accident or a surgery will be given medication by their doctor that makes pain go away. Aspirin and ibuprofen are mild painkillers. Parents sometimes give these medicines to children if they have a headache or a muscle ache (a "growing pain"). You should never take these without your parent knowing about it. But the kinds of painkillers that are prescribed by doctors for adults are much stronger and should never be taken by children because they can do a lot of damage to a child's body.

Practice Saying "No"

Since you obviously cannot supervise your child twenty-four hours a day, seven days a week, it would be helpful if you could somehow "inoc-ulate" your child to resist taking drugs or drinking alcohol. Well, there is a way.

Believe it or not, role-playing situations, in which you play the role of either a peer or an adult offering alcohol or drugs to your child, can go a long way toward inoculating your child against alcohol and drug use. It is even more effective if you begin it at an early age. Here's how to do it:

After you talk with your child about one of the above drugs—let's use the example of alcohol—ask how she or he would respond if a friend or an adult were to offer or suggest using it. Make sure your child understands that "No thanks!" is the appropriate response. Next, engage your child in the following sequence:

PARENT: Let's pretend that I am an adult and I say to you, "Would you like to taste my beer [or wine]?" What would you say?

CHILD: No thanks! [*Make sure your child says this loudly and clearly*].

PARENT: Let's try it again. Suppose I say "It's okay for you to try this. Are you sure you don't want to?"

CHILD: "I said no thanks! Goodbye!" [*Have your child say the words loudly and clearly and then walk away from you*].

Some parents seem to think that role-playing such as the above is silly or not likely to work. In truth, while posting signs in schools which read "Just Say No" is not a very effective drug-prevention strategy, actually practicing *saying* no has been shown to work for adults who wish to stop drinking. And it can work for your child as well.

Drug-Proof Your House

If you have children, chances are you do not leave poisonous substances in places where the children can easily get to them. You know well enough to keep bleach, drain cleaners, and other toxic chemicals in a safe place that you child does not have access to. Why, then, would you want to keep prescription medicines anywhere that your child has access to? As obvious as that seems, many children and teens die every year after getting into their parents' medicine cabinets and swallowing either sleeping pills or painkillers with an alcohol chaser. If you doctor has prescribed such medicines for you, it is worth going to the trouble of buying a lock box to keep them in. Do not assume that your child is ignorant (or not curious) about what is in your medicine cabinet. Here is a tragic example of what can happen:

Zach was one of those teens whose life was adrift. His parents divorced when he was ten. At first he spent most weekends with his father, but by the time a year had passed this had been diluted to about once a month. Then his father met a woman who had two children of her own. After they moved in together Zach saw his father even less often.

Then Zach's mother was seriously injured in a car accident. She went on disability and had to cope with serious chronic pain. Her condition not only made her unable to work but affected her ability to do the day-to-day things she'd always had no trouble with: things like cooking, cleaning, and attending Zach's baseball games.

Zach started drinking at age ten. By the time he was thirteen he was drinking several times a week and smoking pot three or four times a week. Neither of his parents had any idea. He rarely saw his father, and his mother's disability kept her from being able to supervise him with any regularity. It was easy for him to stay away from the house, or even drink in the house without his mother knowing.

Sometimes Zach would get high before going to school. Previously a solid A or B student, he was now a C student, at best, with several D's on his report card. On the weekends he would hang out with friends and drink. He began to show a cynical, sarcastic side to his personality. His teachers, at an annual conference with Zach's parents, described him as "doing nothing" in school.

Although his mother did not drink herself, it wasn't difficult for Zach and his friends to get alcohol. His mother would typically go to bed by 9 p.m., weekends included. That left Zach and his friends to do whatever they wanted to do. On one occasion Zach took his mother's car keys and drove with a friend several miles to a spot in the woods where they met other teens and drank and got high. His mother had no idea he had done this.

It would be a good bet to say that Zach was *self-medicating* with alcohol and marijuana. In other words, he was burying any feelings of depression and anger related to his parents' divorce and his weak relationships with both of them beneath the haze of alcohol and pot.

One night, after waiting for his mother to fall asleep, Zach raided the medicine chest where she kept her pain medications. She had been prescribed powerful opioids, similar to heroin. He and a friend each swallowed a pill and then drank some beer. But while the friend opted to stop at one pain pill, Zach swallowed many more, then drank a few more beers.

The last time his friend saw Zach alive was when Zack got up and stumbled out of the back door of his mother's house. He mumbled something about going to sleep in his mother's car. That was where his friend and his mother found Zach, dead, the next morning.

Most teens know someone like Zach. Most teens also know someone who has died or been seriously injured as a result of alcohol or drug use. What most parents don't know is that these youths usually start drinking and using drugs *before* they reach adolescence. Zach's death was ruled accidental. But Zach was living a life without meaning or direction, and he did not hold life itself in high regard, since he was so willing to take such great risks with it.

Sadly, Zach's mother was not able to make the connection between the behaviors she was seeing and alcohol and drug use. She was not alone in this—parents are often the last to learn the truth.

Summing Up

The idea of children drinking and using drugs is something that doesn't cross the mind of many parents. Hopefully this chapter has enlightened you. What separating parents need to appreciate is the fact that child and teen drug use is correlated with certain *risk factors*. The more risk factors apply to a particular child, the greater the risk. Children of divorce as a group have more of these risk factors, the three most prominent ones being increased stress, anxiety or depression, and less parental supervision.

There is reason why your child should be one of those who falls victim to substance abuse or addiction. The guidelines presented here can help you do this.

Part Five

The Three Crucial Years: *Ages Twelve to Eighteen*

The primary developmental task of the years spanning from pre-adolescence through adolescence is the development of a personal sense of identity: Who I am, what I stand for, and what my future will look like. It is during our teen years that we assess our competencies, develop a sense of where we fit in the social scheme of things, clarify what our values are, and set our expectations for the future.

Once formed, identity can easily turn a life into a self-fulfilling prophecy. Identity emerges through our significant relationships, including our relationships with parents, peers, teachers, and other significant adults in our lives. Clearly, parents' influence on extends beyond a child's early years. Moreover, divorce can represent a serious distraction for parents of teens during these crucial years.

Chapter 21

Understanding Identity

There is a belief in our society that divorce takes its greatest toll on younger children and that, conversely, it has relatively little effect once a child reaches adolescence. This mistaken belief is based on a faulty assumption; namely that a child's development is pretty much complete by the time he or she hits adolescence. Unfortunately, nothing could be further from the truth.

The fact is that adolescence coincides with a major developmental task—one that is as important as security and exploration are in infancy and toddlerhood, and as important as literacy and socialization are in childhood. That developmental task is the emergence of our identity as individuals: That inner sense of who I am and where my life is going. Identity encompasses things such as values and goals, expectations and self-assessments. These are things that younger children are only vaguely in touch with, although we can infer their existence to some extent by how younger children treat others, how they approach challenges, and so on.

Adding to the challenge of parenting adolescents during this crucial developmental stage is the fact that adolescents today exist within a subculture of their own. This subculture has its own rules and tends to be largely hidden from the larger adult culture. It is a culture that is dominated by cell phones and texting, by Internet social networking sites such as Facebook, by camera phones, and by instant messages (IMs). Although teens keep in touch with one another throughout the day through these means, much of their day-to-day lives are a mystery to their parents.

Most parents of teens attest to the fact that as they enter adolescence their children gradually reveal less and less of themselves. This situation tends to worsen when parents decide to separate when their children are teens. Within the teen culture, children of divorce and children who live in blended families are distinct subgroups. Although teens don't talk a lot to their parents, they do talk a lot about their lives with one another. In particular, teens will share with each other those stresses and frustrations that they don't feel free, for one reason or another, to share with their parents.

Divorcing parents will complain that they have to pry even minimal information out of their teens, and that their efforts to find out what is going on their teenager's minds or going on in their lives is often met with either passive resistance ("Nothing much") or an active rebuff ("Get out of my life!"). When parents divorce, teens often respond by hiding behind a common cover story: "I'm fine, just leave me alone."

All parents of adolescents know that the peer group exerts a strong influence on their teenagers. Viewed from the outside perspective of a parent, it may appear that all teens act and think pretty much the same way. But what most parents may not appreciate is that beneath that surface of sameness is an ongoing struggle to find an identity as an individual. And as daunting a task as it may seem, parents of teens can and should seek to exert an influence on that process.

What Is Identity?

Interactions with adults can have a profound effect on a teen's emerging sense of self, either positive or negative. In other words, to some extent the difference between a bully, an underachiever, a self-mutilator, or an alienated youth, as opposed to an All-American kid, has a lot to do with the expectations teens have for themselves, which are formed by the way they are treated and the experiences they have.

One of the most dramatic examples of how even a single experience can help to mold identity and change the course of a teenager's life can be found in *The Autobiography of Malcolm X*. In it, Malcolm recounts a powerful moment when, as an adolescent, his emerging identity apparently was altered by a single interaction. He was in high school and doing very well. One day after class, Malcolm had an interaction with his English teacher.

The teacher asked Malcolm, who was an exceptional student, what his future plans were. Malcolm replied that he was thinking about becoming a lawyer. The teacher laughed. He then offered the advice that, because he was black, Malcolm should think about something "practical," like becoming a carpenter.

This interaction, which screamed out loud to the adolescent Malcolm about the limited expectations he ought to have, coming from an influential adult, altered the course of his life. It was an experience he apparently did not share at the time with anyone who could have done something to soften its impact on his emerging view of himself, and it had a devastating effect on his identity.

Imagine how things might have turned out if, on that fateful afternoon, Malcolm's teacher had opened the doors of possibility instead of closing them. Or imagine how might things have turned out if Malcolm had shared this experience with someone, who saw its implications for his identity, and who responded in a way that would have allowed Malcolm to see it as only one of many alternative directions his life could take?

Alex

Separation and divorce also have the power to strongly influence a teen's expectations for who they can be. Alex was the younger of two sons born to parents who had come from modest beginnings. Alex's father, an ambitious, even driven man, went on to become financially successful as a builder of expensive, custom homes. His mother stayed home to raise Alex and his brother while also becoming active in their community. When Alex entered high school his mother took a part-time job as an aide to their local congressman.

Alex had always enjoyed a comfortable life. He'd grown up in one of the expensive homes that his father had built. A seventeen he had a nice car that he used to drive to school. He was a good student, and was also popular and athletic. In addition to being co-captain of his high school basketball team, he enjoyed golf and tennis, and took private lessons in both. He was beginning to think about what private college he would want to attend. Then the proverbial rug got pulled out from under him.

First, Alex was told that his parents were getting a divorce. His mother explained that part of the divorce settlement was that she and Alex would remain in the house until he graduated. Then the house would be sold. She planned to purchase a condominium with her share of the proceeds, and told Alex that it would be large enough for him and his brother to have their own bedrooms. Meanwhile, Alex's father would temporarily move into one of his unsold houses. As far as she knew, nothing else would change, and life for Alex would go on as it had.

The news shocked Alex. He'd had no idea that there were any problems in his parents' marriage. Neither had his brother, who at that point was finishing his senior year in college. He knew that his father worked long hours, and that his mother often had to attend meetings in the evening and weekends as part of her job, which meant that his parents didn't always spend a lot of time together. But when they were all together Alex had never sensed much tension.

Next, Alex learned that his father was actually divorcing his mother in order to be with another woman. This woman was a professional who also had two children, a boy and a girl, who were not yet teens. Alex had decidedly mixed feelings about this. It was one thing to have to cope with the idea that his family was splitting up; it was another thing altogether to contemplate having to get to know his father's girlfriend and her children. He really had no interest in doing so, and although he'd always had a good relationship with his father, Alex dreaded the day his father would ask him to meet them.

The third and final blow came when a severe and sudden economic turndown hit Alex's father's company, hard. Within a few months, the unsold house that Alex's father had moved into became only one of many expensive houses that he had built on speculation. The buyers for these expensive houses seemed to evaporate overnight.

Like many builders, Alex's father depended on his homes being sold in a reasonable time in order to provide him with cash flow to build more homes. Suddenly, though, the cash flow dried up, and Alex's father went from being financially flush to being a struggling businessman who was severely strapped for cash.

This chain of events happened at the very time when Alex was in the midst of assessing his own future. In the span of a few months he went from being a rich kid who enjoyed a very comfortable lifestyle to the son of a likely bankrupt father who was divorcing his mother in order to live with another woman. He went from someone who could go to any expensive private college he chose—and have friends who enjoyed life's amenities as he did—to having to compete for a spot in his state's public college system.

Alex's father sunk into a sullen depression as a result of his business's failure. Alex saw him rarely, and when he did his blatant pessimism made

Alex anxious. Soon Alex began to feel depressed himself. He broke up with his girlfriend and started withdrawing from his friends.

At that point Alex's mother stepped in. She had known hardship in her life before, had found a way to rise above it, and was not intimidated by it. Indeed, she was a *resilient* individual who staunchly refused to give in to pessimism. She opened the door to a dialogue with Alex about how he was feeling and what he was thinking, particularly about what the future might hold for him. At one point she sat him down, looked him straight in the eye, and said, "Alex, this crisis will not destroy us. Not me, and not you. We may have less money, but we have no less talent, no less ability, and no less potential. Believe me, you will be just fine."

Five years later, when Alex graduated college with a degree in pharmacy, he still remembered that conversation with his mother. Between that conversation and the personal qualities that his mother modeled, you could argue that Alex's identity—and in turn his future—were shaped.

Identity and Behavior

As the above examples show, identity is formed by experience, but in turn identity influences our experience. Think of identity as being the *lens* through which we view the world. Experiences of success, and being held in high regard by others, cause us to build one type of lens through which we then view the world. In contrast, it isn't hard to imagine through what kind of lens the "juvenile delinquent," the "mentally ill" teen, or the "addicted" teen sees the world.

Another lesson to be learned from the above is that you, as a parent, are in a position to exert a strong influence on your teenager's emerging identity. Moreover, as a separated parent you can influence whether your child sees this separation as a tragedy or as an unfortunate crisis that will not dim the possibilities for a bright future.

As children move into adolescence and begin to fashion an identity, that identity will increasingly determine their behavior. At the same time, the rewards and punishments that may have worked well when your child was younger become less and less effective. Most parents are aware of this change, but not the reasons for it.

As an example, consider aggressive behavior. Young children can be taught to cease aggressive behavior using the techniques described in earlier chapters, such as setting limits, redirecting, and using discipline as needed. As many parents and other authorities can attest, these techniques do not work nearly as well with adolescents. That's because aggressive behavior in a teenager is more likely to reflect that teen's emerging identity as a *tough* person. Only if we can get that teen to modify his or her identity—to see him- or herself as a person who prefers to use methods other than aggression as a means of getting what he or she wants, or of resolving conflicts—will this teen will become less aggressive. Until (and unless) that shift in identity occurs, punishing that teen for being aggressive is not likely to prove very effective. At best, the punishment may temporarily suppress aggression. However, if the teen continues to perceive the world as a threatening place in which only the tough survive, the aggressive approach to life will soon reemerge.

As the parent of a teenager, you have a responsibility to instruct. You need, for instance, to teach your son or daughter proper manners and the rules of social etiquette. You need to monitor the clothing they wear and teach them what is acceptable and what is unacceptable. And so on. But you also need to be aware of the *expectations* you communicate to them, and the fact that your *relationship* with them is as important to their development as is the *instruction* you give them. When that relationship changes (for instance, as Alex experienced his relationship with his father changing), it can in turn affect your child's identity, especially if your child interprets the change to mean that he or she is less important or valued.

If your teen begins to act in ways that trouble you, the place to begin looking for a cause is their emerging sense of who they are—in other words, their *identity*. This part of the book will help you do that.

Identity and Divorce

When separation and divorce coincides with a child moving from childhood into adolescence, that fact in and of itself can have an influence on that teen's developing identity. However, since our national divorce rate is high, being the child of divorced parents no longer carries the stigma it once did.

To get a feeling for the stigma that divorce once created, and how divorce could affect a teen's identity, remember the term "broken family." That is the expression that was once commonly applied to children whose parents were divorced. How would it feel to be the product of a "broken" family? Does it make you feel good about yourself? Does it make you feel that not just your family, but *you* as well, may be "broken" or defective somehow? What does it say about your prospects for being happy in the future if your family is "broken"? One silver lining is that your children will not have to carry this stigma.

Glancing Backward to Move Forward

Before we move on, this may be a good moment to reflect on your own childhood and adolescence. Doing so can give you a leg up when it comes to understanding what your teenager is going through, and how your separation might impact the identity process

By answering the questions below as they pertain to you, it will probably quickly become apparent that your emerging identity—your sense of who you were—was a much more powerful determiner of what you did or didn't do than were any specific rewards or punishments that may have been doled out by your parents or teachers. That isn't to say that you didn't like being rewarded (or dislike being punished), but only that these consequences tended to have less of an influence on your behavior once your identity emerged.

Think back to your high school years. Visualize yourself if you can: the clothes you wore, the way you groomed your face and hair, and who you hung out with. Now, answer the following questions for yourself:

- What did you like most about the way you looked?
- Was there something you wished you could change about the way you looked? If so, what was it?
- What did you like most about your personality? Was there something about your personality that you wished you could change? What was it?
- Were you more outgoing, or shy? Did you have a lot of friends, or very few?
- What talents and abilities did you have? What were you best, and worst, at?
- Did you think of yourself as smart?
- Did you believe that you had many options for what you could do as an adult?
- In general, did the future look bright to you, or not so bright?

Your answers to the above questions can provide you with a thumb-nail sketch of your emerging identity as a teenager. Thinking back, how much of your behavior, and how many of your decisions, during those years were influenced by that inner sense you had of who you were? Did you talk much with your parents or any other adults about your sense of who you were?

Taking these few minutes to glance back on your own adolescence can be a good starting point for how you relate to your son or daughter as she moves into this next developmental stage. As she or he emerges from adolescence you can be sure that some sense of identity will have crystallized, and that this identity can exert a strong influence through-out the rest of your child's life.

The Elements of Identity

In some respects identity is a complex thing. It includes the way we see the world, our expectations (for others and for ourselves), and many other components. However, when talking with parents and teens about identity, I (and they) have found it helpful to break it down into three basic questions. These questions are:

- Who am I?
- What do I stand for?
- Where am I going?

The answers that a person comes up with to these questions, when taken together, provide a pretty accurate picture of what a person's iden-tity is. The following chapters will explore each of these questions so as to help you not only understand what kind of identity your teen may be developing, but how you can exert a positive influence of your teenager's emerging identity.

Chapter 22

Helping Teens Answer the Question: *Who Am I?*

A sense of who I am as a person is the first of the three cardinal elements of identity. Teens as a group tend to be relatively noncommunicative about this aspect of identity, and divorcing parents can find themselves too distracted to take the time to open a dialogue about it. However, this inner sense of *"Who am I?"* can have profound implications for a teen's future. This chapter guides you in how to open a dialogue with your teenager about who they are, as well as how to encourage them to broaden this aspect of their identity. As the example in the previous chapter of Alex showed, this can be vital during a period of separation and divorce. One can only imagine how Alex's life might have been altered had he not been able to have such a dialogue with his mother.

Temperaments

One aspect of who we are has to do with our temperaments. These are parts of your personality that you are essentially born with. Sometimes we may not like our own temperaments. Shy people, for instance, often resent their own shyness, and some even hate themselves for it.

Some of the more common temperaments are listed below. As you go through them, think of both yourself and your teenager. What temperaments best describe you, and which ones describe your teen. Don't be surprised if your child is like you in some ways, but very different from you in others. Many people say that their teenager's temperament most resembles that of a grandparent, uncle, or cousin.

The second thing you can do as the parent of an adolescent is to bring this issue of temperament out into the open. Basically this means being able to talk openly about your temperament as well as that of your child. Saying something like: "*We both tend to be on the shy side,*" or "*You are definitely more of a spontaneous person than I am!*" not only makes these differences acceptable, but can actually help your teen develop a more refined sense of who she or he is.

Defining Temperaments

This exercise can be quite illuminating. Beyond that it can mark the opening of a dialogue between you and your teen about this subject of identity. While we all know that we can, as individuals, exhibit any number of different behaviors, depending to some extent on the situation we are responding to, it is also true that each of us has a personality that is defined by certain traits and temperaments that describe who we are *most of the time.*

To complete this exercise, go through the following sets of traits. Each set describes a *dimension* on which people's personalities can differ, from one extreme to another. For each dimension listed, use an *X* to indicate what, in your opinion, best describe first *you* and then *your teen*—in others words, how you and your teen are *most of the time.* (*Note:* Use two different color pens or pencils to denote your temperament versus that of your teen).

If you believe that your and your teen's personalities include the traits at each end of a dimension in approximately equal measure, then place your *X's* in the middle. On the other hand, if you think your personality falls more toward one end, whereas your teen's falls more to the other side, place your *X's* where you think they best describe each of you.

To make this exercise most meaningful, either do it together with your teenager and then discuss the results, or do it yourself and then ask your teen to respond to your estimates of your temperaments. Use the questions that follow the inventory as a guide.

Inventory of Temperaments

Shy ----------------------------------Outgoing
Cautious ------------------------------Risk-Taker
Spontaneous --------------------------Planner
Thick-Skinned ------------------------Thin-Skinned
Athletic ------------------------------Intellectual
Active---------------------------------Sedentary
Competitive---------------------------Cooperative
Confrontational -----------------------Accommodating
Artistically inclined-------------------Mechanically inclined

If you have completed this exercise with your teen, take a few moments to discuss the following:

- How accurate do each of you think the other's self-assessment is?
- On which dimensions do you think the other is "spot on" about how your teen sees him- or herself?
- On which dimensions do you and your teen see yourselves and each other differently?

Temperaments and Interests

One thing about temperaments that is important to keep in mind is that if we follow our temperament it will tend to lead us naturally to our interests. A shy teenager, for example, is less likely than a more social peer to form a strong interest in activities that require a great deal of social interaction. Instead, the shy teen will naturally tend to gravitate toward interests, such as reading or puzzles, that can be pursued by the individual. Similarly, a teenager who enjoys risk-taking and competition is much more likely to pursue downhill skiing or surfing than a teen who prefers a more cautious approach to life and who prefers cooperation to competition. The latter may take to being a collector or an inventor, or may become an "expert" in one or more areas of interest. As adults a shy and cautious person is likely to stick with one job for a long period of time, whereas more spontaneous and risk-taking individuals may change jobs many times.

Despite the obvious connection between temperaments and interests, many teens try to force themselves to embrace an identity that does not really suit them well. This usually reflects the influence of their peer group and the larger culture. Again, it is easy for parents to miss this since teens are typically secretive. It is only through observing your teen and trying to ascertain if your teen is really *enjoying* what he or she is doing that you can get a clue as to whether the interests being pursued match the temperament that lies behind them. There are few things more exhilarating for a parent to witness than the exuberance of a teenager avidly pursuing an interest that suits that teen's personality. In contrast, there is nothing sadder to witness than a teen who is trying to remake him- or herself into the proverbial square peg so as to fit into some square hole.

Keep the Dialogue Going

Over time, as you are able to open a dialogue on the subjects of temperaments and interests, you will be able to get a pretty good sense of how your teen feels about him- or herself and gain important insight into how your teen feels about the temperament he or she was born with. This can be productive for several reasons. Let's look at each in turn:

- *There are two sides to every coin.*
  Let's take a temperament such as shyness. While your teen may not like this aspect of temperament, shy people tend to be sensitive and reflective people, which can be viewed as a personal asset, not a liability. As a parent you are in a position to point this out if and when your teenager expresses dissatisfaction at being shy. This is not the same as simply saying "*It's okay to be shy.*" Bromides like this usually offer little solace. That would be like saying to a basically noncompetitive adolescent that "*It's okay to not be competitive,*" when most of his or her peers seem to be respected for their competitiveness. Rather than saying something like this, it is better to offer the observation that people who prefer cooperation over competition are frequently the most successful in life over the long run. For example, the most effective corporate executives are those who are able to inspire teamwork and cooperation over competition. As a third example, consider people who are prone to being interpersonally sensitive (so-called thin-skinned). These

same people also tend to be empathic types. Again, a teen might not like being thin-skinned; on the other hand, the idea of being empathetic is not such a bad thing.

- *You can change (within limits).*

A second advantage to being able to talk to your teen about temperaments is that there are things that a person *can* do to help compensate for a temperament they wish they could change. Consider the temperament of shyness we have been talking about. Shy teens may never be able to totally transform themselves into "Miss or Mister Congeniality." However, there are ways to work on being less shy. Programs such as Toastmasters are designed to help shy people overcome their shyness enough to be able to speak in public. And self-help books are available that teach shy people skills they can use so as to feel more comfortable in social situations.

One school social worker came up with an innovative idea to tackle this issue. She decided that the best thing to do was to bring the issue of shyness out into the open to make it less of a "big deal," and at the same time offering students an opportunity to work on reducing their shyness. The high school she worked in had its own television studio, which it used to broadcast a brief "morning update" to every classroom at the start of the school day. Naturally, it was the more outgoing students who signed up to do the daily news and sports updates, conduct interviews, and read announcements.

The social worker arranged to be interviewed on the subject is shyness. During the interview she pointed out that a great many people regarded themselves as shy. Moreover, she said, she was starting a "Shy Persons Institute" in the school. The Institute was to meet every other Wednesday after school. It would feature lectures from community leaders, athletes, professionals, and others, all of whom regarded themselves as shy but who were nonetheless successful. The Institute would also offer students opportunities to work on reducing their shyness. One very successful technique involved teaching students the art of puppetry. As it turns out, many successful puppeteers are shy people. But by speaking through a puppet they are able to overcome their shyness. If they do this long enough, there is a spill-over effect into the social arena. The Institute proved to be very popular, and this social worker believed that it helped quite a few students overcome any shame they had about being shy, as well as helping them overcome their shyness to a degree.

If you as a parent know how your teen feels about his or her temperaments, you will be in a position to be supportive and make useful suggestions on how your teen can work on changing something he or she would like to change.

- *Avoiding the "square peg/round hole" dilemma.*
We've already touched on this issue. The problem here is that only a minority of teens will be open and honest about the qualities in themselves that they like the least. More likely, they will identify a peer whose qualities they admire and then strive to remake themselves in the image of that peer. The advice offered above, about shyness, can go a long way toward reducing the chances that your teenage son or daughter will do this. That said, it is still important that you regularly reinforce the idea that you really do like the personality and temperament that your child has (despite whatever quarrels you may have!) and that you are a firm advocate of pursuing interests and goals that are consistent with that personality, as opposed to having your teen try to remake him-or herself. Life is too full of stories of adults who end up leading the life their parents (or some other influential adult) chose for them, or which they falsely believed would lead to admiration from peers, as opposed to pursuing interests that were more in tune with their innate temperaments. Maintaining a dialogue with your teen through these crucial years can help prevent this.

Talents

A second, equally important piece of our identity is our sense of what we are good at: our talents and abilities. Some talents—just like some temperaments—are more valued by society than others, and as a result society tends to steer youths in these directions and reward them when they do so. This may serve society's needs, but it does not always make for a good fit for the individual. When I was a teen, for example, engineering was considered a prestigious career track. As a result many bright young men and women chose to go in that direction, partly due to the social status of the job, and partly due to the financial security that comes from an engineers' salary. However, a fair number of these young men and women had to struggle just to get through a course of study in engineering, and ended up performing only marginally on the job. Others ended up in a career that was not a good match for their temperaments or interests. These included people who might have been happier pursuing careers in teaching, for example, or in the medical professions (or psychology!). In choosing a career path, therefore, it is important that parents encourage their teenage sons and daughters to consider their interests, their temperaments, *and* their talents.

As a parent you have no doubt been aware of not only your child's temperament, but his or her interests and talents, for many years now. Hopefully your teen has already had some experience pursuing interests and getting in touch with some of his or her abilities. This sense of what he or she likes and is good at forms the kernel of this aspect of identity. As the parent of an adolescent you can play an important and influential role in developing your teen's identity in this area. What follows are some suggestions for doing this.

- *New experiences as a way to open the door to an expanded identity.*
  There is no way for a teen to discover that she or he has a talent is there is no opportunity to explore it. That in itself is one reason why it is a bad idea for school systems to eliminate co-curricular activities when they face budget constraints. Parents sometimes view such activities—sports, clubs, drama, and so on—as "frills" that are not essential to the mission of the school system. They often feel the same way about courses in art and music. But by eliminating these from the overall curriculum they are reducing students' opportunities to discover who they are and what pathways may be open to them for the future. Many successful actors and artists, for example, first discovered their talents in high school.

  As was stated at the outset of this book, divorcing parents may face financial constraints even greater that the average family. Money for co-curricular activities may be increasingly difficult to come by. One resource available to you is your community. Check with your local town offices to see what may be offered, either free or for little money. These are most often offered through the local recreation department and include offerings for all age groups, from children through adults. I recommend you get yourself on the mailing for announcements of such programs. Go through them and encourage your child to try out something new starting as young as possible. Do not, of course, pressure your child to participate. Gentle encouragement should be as far as you go.

- *Challenge and adventure as ways to open the door to an expanded identity.*
  Unfortunately, as far as many families get to a true family adventure or challenge is five days at a theme park or on a cruise ship. When divorce strikes, funds for such adventures may be decidedly limited. There is no denying that such vacations can be enjoyable. They are a time for the family to be together and engage in something other than their day-to-day routines. As much fun as they can be, though, such experiences are rarely true adventures; nor do they typically offer anything more challenging than waiting on long lines for admission. And often families end up splitting apart as they pursue different interests, reuniting only at prearranged times.

  By "challenge" and "adventure" I am referring to activities that engage the entire family in the same activity; activities that offer some element of discovery and that require teamwork. Examples would include family camping trips or exploring national parks together. Taking a three or four-hour hike as a family, bringing along backpacks loaded with food and drink, to explore a place that none of them have ever seen before, serves multiple purposes. First, it helps bond the family together. This is as true for divorced parents and their children as it is for two-parent families. In fact, engaging in such activities through the divorce process can go a long way toward reducing stress and allowing your child to continue on a healthy developmental track.

  Another thing that family adventures can do is instill a spirit of healthy adventure in children and teens. Since they do not know precisely what they will find in the course of their adventure, these family treks offer breaks in the predictability of everyday life. They afford opportunities for children and teens to discover something new about the world, and perhaps about themselves. One teen, for example, who went with his parents on a two-day river rafting expedition, discovered an interest in nature and the outdoors that affected his life. He went on to college to study forestry and became a teacher and part-time park ranger.

Who You Are versus Who You Should Be

In helping to expand your teen's sense of who she or he *is*, it's important that you as a parent try not to inject too much of your opinions about who you think your teen *should* be. This may be harder to do than it sounds, because most parents do have aspirations for their children and, as parents, we often have opinions about what our children should not grow up to be. I am referring to our biases about what we think of as that counts as "success." For example, many parents would probably approve of their teenager expressing a desire to become a doctor or a lawyer. In contrast, depending on their own aspirations for their child, they might not feel the same way if their teenager expressed a desire to become an electrician, an artist, or (as in the example cited above) a park ranger.

One factor that appears to govern parents' ideas about who their children should be is a desire to see their children enjoy a better life than they as parents have. By "better" I mean both financially and more satisfying. If anything, the strain of divorce can exacerbate this tendency, especially if the divorce has created financial stress. As well intentioned as they may be, parents can undermine their children's self-esteem and cause them to feel conflicted about their very identity if they pressure their children hard to develop certain skills and abilities while ignoring others. One adult woman, for example, complained that from the moment her parents divorced, when she was nine years old, both of them persistently pressured her to pursue math and business, despite the fact that her greater interest by far was in literature. In retrospect she believed they did this because chronic financial hardship was one factor that contributed to the failure of her parents' marriage. Though she had an obvious talent for writing, she believed that neither parent saw any way to translate that into academic success. This woman went on to a career as an executive in which she was financially successful but very unhappy. It was only years later, through personal counseling, that she "rediscovered" her initial interest and talents, and went on to a second career as a college teacher and professional writer.

The moral of this story is that separation and divorce often causes parents to worry about the future of their teenage sons and daughters. Such anxiety can easily get translated into concerns about the direction that a teen may be going in, along with efforts to "steer" that teen in a direction the parent thinks is best. Despite their best intentions, such efforts can distort a teen's emerging identity and can even lead a teen to make choices that are not a good fit for who they really are.

Summing Up

While it is fine for you as a parent to have some ideas about what "success" means to you, your child's overall development will proceed best if you take the position of helping him or her discover as much as possible about who he or she is, in terms of temperaments, interests, and talents, and then allow your child to carve out his or her own identity based on that knowledge. Following the exercises in this chapter can help you avoid some of the parenting pitfalls that separation and divorce can create.

Chapter 23

Helping Teens Answer the Question: *What Do I Stand for?*

Values and priorities—what we as individuals stand for—represent the second of three elements of identity. It is not until they approach adolescence that boys and girls are able to talk meaningfully about values. Prior to that, a child's behavior is governed primarily by more or less rigid codes of conduct—ideas about "right" versus "wrong" things to do. At this earlier developmental stage rewards and punishments are effective ways of shaping and controlling children's behavior. There is also a genuine need for certain hard-and-fast rules of behavior, such as not using physical violence to settle conflicts, not lying, not riding a bicycle without a helmet, not stealing from others, and so on. This is not to say that younger children do not have a sense of fairness, which they do; but they only learn to articulate their values and priorities as they become teens.

However, as children move into adolescence most parents begin to note that rewards and punishments start losing some of the power they once had to control behavior. Moreover, if hard-and-fast rules are not instilled in a child by the time she or he reaches adolescence, it becomes very difficult to instill them at all. It's akin to closing the barn door after the horse has run away.

Rewards and punishments begin to lose their power as values and priorities begin to crystallize. As this process unfolds, values and priorities exert an increasing influence on the decisions a child makes and on how he or she behaves. The question that parents of teens always seem to ask is: *"What accounts for how my son or daughter is behaving?"* The answer is: *"The behavior you are seeing reflects your teen's underlying identity, including their sense of who they are as well as their personal values and priorities."*

Value, Priorities, and Divorce

If you want to understand your teenager's attitudes and behavior, you need to understand that these reflect in large part who your teen thinks she or he is *plus* his or her emerging values and priorities. In the previous chapter we looked at the role you can play in influencing your teen's sense of self, as well as the effects that separation can have on this aspect of identity. Specifically, you learned that you can help your teen to expand and clarify his or her emerging identity by talking about temperaments, exposing your teen to new experiences, and fostering opportunities for adventure and challenge. You learned that the stress of divorce can lead you to try to steer your teen in a direction that may strike you as best, but that does not in fact suit his or her personality. The parent who succeeds in doing this may relieve their own anxiety but may well be steering their teen down the pathway to unhappiness.

Let's turn our attention now to the issue of values and priorities, the role these things play in identity, and how separation and divorce can affect them. And let's begin again with an example.

Lauren

On some level Lauren, who was now sixteen, always knew that her parents were very different people. Her father, Paul, was a landscape architect who loved his work but was not particularly ambitious to get ahead. Because of that, and partly because of the nature of his business, Paul had twice been laid off, both times as a result of economic turndowns. It seemed that the kind of work Paul was best at was something that companies were willing to pay for in good times, but not so willing to pay for in bad times.

Lauren described her father as funny and warm. He loved nature, and he loved to hike and bike. He took his job seriously, but he could also be laid back, and Lauren got the impression that work was not necessarily the most important thing in her father's life. He had modest needs, and he was a founding member of their town's conservation committee.

Lauren's mother, Carly, was cut from an altogether different cloth. The daughter of working-class parents whom Lauren described as rather severe and difficult to warm up to, Carly could be described as an "over-achiever." As compared to Paul she was anything but laid back. An attorney, she had worked hard to become a partner in a large law firm. Like her husband she took care of her health; but whereas Paul was happy to take a hike in the woods, Carly jogged almost every day, had a personal trainer, and worked out three times a week in a gym. Her work matched her personality and could be described in one word: intense.

Lauren, an only child, had also long been aware of a certain degree of tension between her parents. She knew that they wanted different things. Her mother, for example, spoke often and loudly about wanting a larger house, and also about wanting to buy a second home in an expensive resort area. She often bought herself tasteful and expensive jewelry, and her professional wardrobe was similarly tasteful and expensive: designer label suits and Italian shoes.

Paul, in contrast to Carly, was content to wear the same kinds of clothes—tweed jackets and cotton pants—that he had worn twenty years earlier as a graduate student in architecture school. While his wife drove an expensive sports car, he liked his old boxy Volvo. He always replied to his wife's statements about a new house by explaining that he was comfortable in their home and did not see need for a larger one. Also, his ideal vacation was to visit and explore a place he'd never been to, and he saw no need for a vacation home. If they did buy one, he argued, he and Carly would feel obligated to vacation there all the time.

Despite her awareness of these differences, like most teens Lauren was surprised when her parents informed her that they were separating. She was all the more surprised because her father had recently found another job. What she later surmised, though, was that her mother had simply waited, not wanting to kick a person when he was down, as the saying goes.

Lauren lived in an upper–middle-class community and attended an upper–middle-class school. She was very much aware that some of her friends were into things like status clothes, nice cars, and fancy electronics, all of which were expensive. While Paul and Carly were together they had managed to reach a compromise in this regard. Although Lauren did own some designer clothes, her wardrobe was decidedly modest as compared to those of some of her friends.

When her parents separated, any previous agreement Lauren's parent may have had with regard to material things quickly went by the wayside. And as she divided her time between two households, the differences between her parents' values and lifestyles became amplified. For instance, after the house was sold, Carly purchased a large and luxurious condominium with amenities that included a heated swimming pool and an elaborate exercise facility. Paul, meanwhile, rented a small house on land that bordered a state park, which offered easy access to hiking and biking trails.

When she was with her mother, Lauren found herself being enticed to go shopping together to the small designer label stores that dotted a nearby upscale mall. When she went to spend her first weekend with her father, on the other hand, he surprised her with an all-but-brand-new parka he'd bought at his favorite consignment store!

Once parents decide to separate, unless they had few differences in values and priorities *before* the separation, any compromises they may have forged in these areas while together are apt to go out the window. This can leave children—like Lauren—caught in the middle of conflicting value systems. This can be very significant for teens, whose emerging identities include the values and priorities that they will live by.

How to Influence Values and Priorities

In the beginning of this book I introduced the notion of the child-centered divorce. By that I meant that if parents can keep their eye on the key developmental tasks facing their children during the first three years following separation, and are ready and able to do what they can to keep their child on a healthy developmental track during those three crucial years, then those children can not only survive divorce but emerge as stronger and more resilient individuals.

The subject of this chapter—values and priorities—is a crucial aspect of adolescent development. In Lauren's case, she said that she enjoyed spending time with her father, and doing things like biking on park trails or canoeing on a lake. At the same time, she admitted that she had expanded her wardrobe considerably in the year following her parents' separation, and that she liked being one of the "in crowd" at school. She much preferred, for example, to invite friends to her mother's upscale condo than to her father's modest house by the woods.

The first key to understanding and influencing your teenager's character development is to understand this simple rule: *behavior reflects values and priorities*. If you follow this simple rule then it will become easier and easier for you to "see" the value or priority that underlies almost anything your teen says or does. Whether it is the clothes they wear, the attitudes they express, whom they choose to associate with, or the things they do, teens' behavior pretty much points directly to this aspect of identity.

The second key to influencing teens' values and priorities is to see how they compare to your own. In the above example, Lauren's parents' lifestyles reflected two very different sets of values and priorities. For Carly, life was about hard work and enjoying the fruits of one's labor. She believed that she worked hard for her money and was entitled to spend it on a good life. Paul also had a work ethic but was much less driven to make money or to acquire material possessions. Lauren, it appeared, was leaning toward embracing her mother's value system. The question here is whether either parent was consciously aware of his or her own value system and how it was affecting their daughter. Would Cindy, for example, truly want Lauren to become materialistic? Or, if she had a choice, would she want to temper materialism with some other value, such as modesty?

If you take the time to listen to the attitudes your teenager expresses, observe the choices he or she makes, and the way he or she behaves, it should not be difficult for you to "connect the dots" between these attitudes, choices, and actions and the values that underlie them. If you are willing to be honest about your own values and priorities, you can then begin to exert your influence on this important aspect of identity development. You can do this in a simple and straightforward way. First, *connect a value to the behavior or attitude you see or hear; second, let your teen know which ones you admire and respect*. Here are some additional guidelines:

- *Disclose and illustrate your own personal values as they are reflected in others' behavior.* Make a point of mentioning people you admire and why, whether they are personal acquaintances or people you read or hear about in the newspaper or on network news. Explain why you admire these people in terms of the values they represent. Example: *"My friend _____ volunteers one day a month at the soup kitchen in town. I admire him for doing that."*

- *Lead by example.* Spend some time thinking about your own values and how these may be reflected in the things you do and the choices you make. Rest assured, your children will be strongly influenced by the example you set, regardless of what they see or hear elsewhere.
- *Don't be shy.* Parents should ask teens what they believe in, if they have given any thought to what goals or aspirations they may have, and what their priorities, values, and goals are. Despite what many adults may think, teens enjoy talking about such matters, especially to adults who are willing to hear them out.
- *Praise your teen when attitudes or behaviors reflect values you admire.* If your teen does volunteer work, raises money for charity, or simply goes out of his or her way to help someone else, point it out and say that you admire that behavior or attitude.

Summing Up

There is altogether too little dialogue these days between parents and teens on the subject of values and how they relate to the attitudes we have, the choices we make, and the things we do. This problem is surely not limited to parents who are divorcing; however, to the extent that divorcing parents have divergent values and priorities, these differences ca become exaggerated, as they were in Lauren's case, following separation. To minimize the internal conflict that this can create in a teen, it is vital that divorcing parents each establish an ongoing dialogue about values and their relation to behavior and choices, as the values your teen embraces now will exert their influence for years to come.

Chapter 24

Helping Teens Answer the Question: *Where Am I Going?*

There is a large and growing body of research that strongly supports the power that expectations have over behavior. Simply put, we often get what we expect. In this third and final area of identity, divorcing parents once again cannot afford to be distracted. Adolescence—and the high school years—are a critical time for setting expectations. These crucial years hold the potential to literally set the course for your child's entire future. Divorce, because it can disrupt so many aspects of family life, can be expected to impact a teen's sense of where his or her life is headed. The risk is that negative expectations that are formed during the three crucial years can turn into a self-fulfilling prophecy.

Gauging Your Teen's Expectations

We've all had the experience of sitting through an inspirational speech and being told to "aim high," or to believe that we can be anything we want to be. Teenagers are singled out for such speeches, and if you've ever observed an auditorium filled with high school students, assembled to listen to such a speech, you know how they look: slumped in their seats, their eyes glazed over. It's hard to identify those who in the audience are truly moved by such speeches (though some in fact are). Most just wait patiently for it to be over. And then there are those who fidget and joke around.

The problem with such motivational speeches is that they have about as much effect on teens' actual expectations for themselves as speeches about drug use have on teens' actual alcohol and drug use. In short, posting a sign saying "Aim High" in the lobby of a high school is about as effective as positing a sign that reads "Drug Free School Zone." Both amount to little more than wishful thinking on the part of school personnel and parents. I say this not to disparage such efforts, but rather to make the point that it takes a lot more than speeches and signs to really influence teens' expectations and behavior.

Teens are notorious for telling adults what they think those adults want to hear, especially if they perceive that those adults are not genuinely interested in hearing what the teens really want to say. You could call these adults "disingenuous" because they are actually more interested in telling teens what they should do (or think) than they are in listening to what teens think they should do (or what they really think). For instance, if an adult who is perceived as disingenuous asks a teen a question like "*What are your expectations for the future?*" what he is likely to get is either no response, or else a canned answer.

If you want to get an idea of your teenager's real expectations, you need to be prepared to hear some unvarnished truths. You also need to "read" his or her behavior.

You can infer that your teen has essentially positive expectations for his or her future if he or she:

- willingly takes on challenges.
- sets and pursues personal goals.
- is generally an optimist.
- cares about his or her appearance.
- gets along with most adults.
- hangs out with peers who are successful, socially and academically.
- appears to be aware of his or her personal talents and abilities.

Here is an example of a teen with positive expectations:

Gina is sixteen and a sophomore in high school. She has always been a responsible student who basically likes school. Her grades are typically As and Bs. She plays soccer in the fall and basketball in the spring. Her goal is to make her high school varsity basketball team. She exercises regularly, has a solid circle of friends, several of whom who spend time in her at home frequently.

Like her peers Gina is *wired:* connected to a social network of her peers via cell phone and the social networking site, Facebook. She enjoys listening to music on the MP3 player she got for her birthday, and is looking forward to turning sixteen so she can get her driver's license. She also has a friend whose mother is a store manager at a local mall, where Gina believes she will be able to get a part-time job. As far as dating is concerned, she has always had a few boys who she regarded as "friends" but has expressed no strong desire as yet to have a "boyfriend." In fact, she has commented to her mother that a couple of girls she knows seem too "dependent" on boys. For instance, she once told her mother that her friend, Emily, "is a good friend, but as soon as she finds a new boyfriend she disappears from my life."

In contrast to Gina, here is a description of behavior that suggests low expectations: Justin, also age 16 and a high school sophomore, was a straight A student through the seventh grade. After that, however, his school performance dropped off precipitously. His teachers were clear: it was not lack of ability, but lack of motivation, that was the cause of this. Justin often fails to hand in assigned homework, and he prepares very little for exams. He has a few close friends, but those he does hang out with tend to be underachievers and known drug users. He is not involved in any school activities and spends most of his time "hanging out" with friends. His current hobby is playing bass guitar. Before that he enjoyed skateboarding, but he has pretty much given that up over the past year. When asked about the future he shrugs and talks vaguely about putting together a band and making a recording. With respect to appearance, Justin prefers a "dark" (though not "gothic") look. His parents describe him as something of a recluse at home. He does not get into conflict with his two siblings, but neither is he exactly "part of the family."

In both of the above cases the teen's behavior speaks volumes. As the parent of a teen you need to be able to connect the dots and read the message in the actions you see. Of these two adolescents, Gina is clearly the one whose life is going somewhere. Justin, in contrast, is pretty much treading water. As you will learn shortly, he is also at risk for substance abuse.

As it happened neither Gina's nor Justin's parents were going through a divorce, although Justin's parents acknowledged their marriage was having its problems. As far as this aspect of identity is concerned—the sense of *Where am I going?*—the differences between these two adolescents is painfully apparent. As much as spouses whose marriage is in turmoil may believe they successfully hide their issues from their children, the reality is that many of the issues that are covered in this book—from bedwetting and school phobia to underachievement and substance abuse—begin to emerge before the actual split. It is during this time and the subsequent three years that parents can successfully intervene so as keep their children on a healthy developmental track and avert long-term negative consequences.

Learned Optimism: How to Talk about High Expectations Without Sounding Phony

We touched on this idea of optimism in the first part of this book, which asked you as a parent to examine some of your own behaviors and attitudes. One of the qualities of a *resilient* personality is optimism: the idea that we can exert some control over our lives and in the process make our lives better.

There are a few life events that severely test a person's resilience. On the top of the list are the death of a loved one, losing one's job, and divorce. This is as true for teens as it is for their divorcing parents. Even teens who have been relatively resilient (such as Gina, described earlier) can have their resilience tested by divorce. This is more true the more your divorce disrupts your teenager's life, with the worst disruption not being a change in overall life style but a forced change in schools.

In 2008, Barack Obama won a presidential election campaign largely with the simple slogan *Yes We Can*. This might seem like naïve wishful thinking, but when embraced by millions this belief led to a landslide victory. So, as simple as it may seem, such an inner belief has great power. It establishes and affirms our expectations. In teens it can literally make the difference between a life of success versus one of failure.

You can expect your teen's response to your divorce to pretty much mirror your own. In effect, children *learn* optimism (versus pessimism) from their parents. This learning begins well before adolescence, and will probably have shown its face before now; for example, in how your teen deals with adversity and how willing he or she is to take on a challenge.

If your teen already has shown signs of holding low expectations for him- or herself, some professional counseling may be necessary to get at the root of your child's pessimism. However, even if this is the case, there are things you can do as a parent to help promote positive expectations and a resilient approach to life in your teenager. Here are two of those ways.

The "Bumpy Road" Technique

Researchers have found that another difference between people who are able to bounce back fairly quickly from a crisis (resilient people) versus those who get thrown off track by it has to do with their overall view of life. Resilient people approach life in a way that is similar to the way elite athletes approach their sport. A member of an elite basketball team, for example, will try his or her best to win each and every game. These athletes are satisfied with nothing less that a one hundred percent effort from themselves. At the same time, if they should lose a game they do not sink into a state of depression or hopelessness. This is because as much as they strive to win, they accept the reality that they may some-times lose. Rather than wasting a lot of time mourning the loss, they turn their attention to the next scheduled game.

You can think of the above as the *bumpy road* view of life. Divorce, losing a job, or getting sick can all be thought of as "bumps" in the road of life. That's not to deny that some "bumps" are a lot bigger than oth-ers; at the same time, if we expect life to have its ups and downs we are much less likely to despair when we do hit a bump.

The opposite of this view could be called the *expressway* view of life. People who hold this view act as if they expect life to be like a trip on an expressway, free of bumps and delays, where you always get to your destination quickly and effortlessly. Whether they want to admit it or not, many people do hold this view of life. It's revealed best in their reac-tion to disappointment and frustration. When faced with these things they act as if life is somehow treating them unfairly. They get depressed and discouraged. Rather than trying harder to overcome adversity they are more likely to give up. Similarly, rather than risking frustration or disappointment they are apt to pursue only those goals that are easily attainable.

The above two views of life are readily apparent in adolescents. Your teenager's expectations—including his or her outlook on life and crises—play a key role in determining the goals he or she sets as well as his or her ability to persevere in the face of adversity. As a divorc-ing parent, you can exert a strong influence in this area. If you perceive your divorce as a setback so severe that you will never overcome it, that attitude may well spill over onto your teenage son or daughter. In contrast, if you approach your divorce as a serious bump in the road of life, but one which you firmly believe you can overcome, that also may spill over. By the same token, you may believe that a result of your divorce is that you will never find happiness again or, alternatively, that after the turmoil settles you will find happiness. Those attitudes, too, can affect your teen.

Hopefully you will have started well before your child reaches adolescence in expressing a life view that is more consistent with the bumpy road perspective than the expressway perspective. If, however, you notice a change in your teen's behavior, and in particular a tendency to give up easily, pursue only minimal goals, and act as if life is hopeless, the culprit may very well a change in his or her overall outlook. Having a dialogue about this can be very helpful.

The "Identity as a Menu" Technique

Identity emerges and crystallizes during adolescence. That identity includes our sense of who we are, what we stand for, and where we think our lives are going. Once it forms, our identity can easily exert a strong influence on how we think, how we perceive the world, and how we act. It can become the road map for how a teen's life will unfold.

Divorce represents a crisis which, depending on how it is handled, can either strengthen or weaken a teen's emerging identity. It is entirely possible for your teenager to emerge from the crisis of divorce as a more resilient individual. Conversely, divorce can contribute to a dysfunctional identity. The difference often hinges on your teen's perception of what the future holds.

Warning signs that a teen may be moving toward a dysfunctional identity include the following:

- An inability to articulate any meaningful personal goals.
- Difficulty naming personal assets, talents, and abilities.
- Minimal or no involvement in co-curricular activities, sports, or organizations.
- Avoidance of challenges.
- Giving up easily in face of frustration.
- Negative self-statements, such as "I'm dumb," or "I'm not one of the popular kids in school."

- Hanging out with under-achievers.
- Neglecting personal hygiene.
- Self-mutilation ("cutting").

If a teen begins to exhibit any of the above traits parents should take note. These behaviors could well be the teen's way of "speaking" through actions, not unlike the way that younger children speak through their actions. Bear in mind, though, that poor personal hygiene is not the same thing as an unconventional taste in clothing. "Goths," for example, dress in dark clothing, may dye their hair jet black, and wear heavy jewelry. "Skaters" like to ear baggy jeans and loose-fitting T-shirts.

Adolescence—at least in healthy teens—is a time of experimentation. Therefore it is *normal* if your teen experiments with different "looks." In fact, these different looks are often a sign that a teen is trying on different identities for size. That's where the *life as a menu* technique comes in.

Adolescence is a time of internal turmoil as much as it is a time of exploration and excitement. On the one hand all teens understand that they are *individuals,* with a unique set of talents, temperaments, and so on. At the same time teens look around them, see a variety of different *groups* and cliques, and eventually gravitate toward one or another.

There are many different identities that could be considered functional. While you as a parent might prefer to see your teen move toward one of these as opposed to another, the fact is that they all can lead to healthy and productive adult lives. Goths, for example, are often unconventional people who have a creative streak and are able to think in unconventional ways. Interestingly, this describes most successful entrepreneurs as much as it describes gothic teenagers.

The monikers that teens use to refer to the various groups that populate America's high schools can be quite diverse, although most teens relate to groups such as: *preppies, jocks, skaters,* and *goths.* One high school junior described the social landscape in her school more simply yet somewhat ominously: "There's the highs, and there's the lows, and the highs pick on the lows and the lows just have to put up with it."

It may strike you as odd that groups such as *druggies, gangstas,* and *cutters* could actually exist, or that they would represent identities that other teens recognize, but they do. In almost every American high school today teens know these groups and who is in them.

All of the above groups can be thought of as *templates* for identity. While a few teens may actually gravitate toward more than one of these groups, most choose only one. This is a two-way process in which the teen first gravitates toward a group that appears to match his or her self-image. Then, once he or she is accepted into one of these groups, a teen increasingly adopts its values and attitudes and begins to act more and more as others in the group do.

Experience teaches that teens will not abandon their affiliation with a peer group simply because they asked to do so, and will be even more resistant to doing so if they are criticized for who they choose to hang out with. This is precisely why even teens who successfully complete a drug rehabilitation program have a high relapse rate. Their first contacts after leaving rehab are almost always with the same group of friends they hung out with when they were using. Even the best of intentions can rarely hold up against this peer pressure. The key to preventing relapse among teens is to try to transition them from a drug-using peer group to a non-drug-using one.

Even allowing for a teen's loyalty to his or her peer group, you as a parent can still have a significant influence on your teen's identity development. The only time you should really be concerned about this process of affiliation is if your teenager seems to be drifting more and more toward a group that you have real concerns about. This is not unheard of among teens whose parents are divorcing. A teen who previously associated mainly with skaters or jocks, for instance, may suddenly spend much less time with that crowd and instead start hanging out with one or two individuals from the drop-out crowd. This "peer group drift" should be a red flag to you that your divorce may be having an effect on your teen's identity development. In that case, rather than going toe to toe with your teen and trying to force a change in peer group, try the following.

Alternative Identities: Trying Identities on for Size

One useful strategy for encouraging a teen to consider identities other than one he or she appears to be drifting toward is to introduce the idea of identities being akin to different sets of clothing: preppy, gothic, jock, skater, and so on. Each of these has their unique "look." Similarly, different peer groups each have a "look": interests, preferences in music, outlook on life, and so on.

When a person changes their "look," they see themselves and the world from a different perspective. By the same token, others see them differently and relate to them differently. One simple but potentially powerful intervention with a teen that follows from this is to ask the teen how he or she would *like* to be perceived and treated by others. Their response is then followed up by asking if the way they dress, the way they act, and the people they hang out with, are consistent with their goal of how they want to be regarded and treated.

When presented in this manner, most teens can relate to this way of looking at identity, since many of them may in fact have already experimented with different looks. At the same time, it introduces the notion that they have a *choice* about who they will be. Rather than coming at them, then, and trying to coerce (or bribe) teens into abandoning a peer group they are either moving toward or already affiliated with, this approach simply suggests to them that a peer group represents only one of many alternative identities that they have the option of pursuing.

Try talking to your teen about "trying on alternative identities on for size," almost as if it were a suit of clothes, before settling on one. Point out that once a person finally does settle on a peer group (and an identity), that decision can exert a strong influence on how that person's life unfolds. Here is an example:

Robin was a beautiful girl of sixteen, and also one who was causing her mother, Karen, to lose a lot of sleep. Robin's father had moved out of the house about a year earlier. This happened following many years of increasingly intense marital conflict. Robin's parents differed over a great many issues including lifestyle (he was a profligate spender, she was an earnest saver), priorities (his motto was *"you only have one life to live, so enjoy it,"* whereas her goal was to build a secure future for her three children), and interests (he liked to play golf as often as possible; she was a devoted jogger).

Robin's changes in behavior actually began shortly before her father left, and they were clearly correlated with her parents' escalating marital unhappiness. The changes that drove Karen's anxiety centered around her daughter's drifting away from old friends and interests, toward new ones that Karen did not feel very good about. This included Robin's decision to cut her long her strawberry blonde hair very short and dye it jet black, and to go from one piercing per ear to four. She also decided, in her words, to "take a break" from the competitive swimming and gymnastics she'd been involved in since age seven. Instead, she spent a lot of time hanging out with new friends, talking on her cell phone, and isolating herself in her room, where she listened to music.

Never a social butterfly, Robin also suddenly appeared to discover an interest in partying. She virtually disappeared on weekends, and when she was home she interacted very little with her mother, brother, and sister. Karen suspected that alcohol was surely a part of the party scene, and probably marijuana as well, at the very least.

In approaching this issue with Robin (who, happily, was quite willing to talk to a counselor), I began by causally asking what group within her school was most associated with her new "look." "The Goths, I suppose," she replied.

"Do you think of yourself as a Goth?" I inquired, to which Robin smiled. "Not really," she said, "but I have a couple of friends who are. I just always wanted to see what it would be like to try on a new look, you know what I mean?"

I nodded. Indeed, having once been an adolescent myself, I did know what Robin meant. Almost all teens, at one point or another, experience some urge to break out of the identity they have been associated with. It is something akin to a "sow your wild oats" urge, and it is a healthy sign that a teen is in the process of working out their identity.

After talking for a while, I was sure that this was Robin's major motivation. At the same time, she admitted that this new group she was experimenting with did use drugs (though she did not) as well as alcohol (which she did, but not often or a lot). She also confided that, although she knew other teens whose parent had divorced, none of those who had been in her former inner circle of friends were children of divorce. This was in contrast to the new friends she was making.

Her reassurances to her mother notwithstanding, it did bother Robin that her family was breaking up. "It makes me feel weird," she said, "It just makes me feel as if the future is no longer certain. Before, I never thought about money, but now I think about it a lot. Will my mother be able to afford to keep us in the house? Will there be money for us kids to go to college?"

In addition, Robin was concerned about her mother. Again, despite assurances to the contrary, from Robin's perspective Karen seemed depressed. "She isn't the same upbeat, happy person I've always known. I realize she has a lot on her mind. I just hope she will be okay."

The good news here is that Robin had not yet embraced an identity change or totally given up her old interests. On the other hand, she did admit to feeling somewhat adrift and uncertain of the future. She was worried about her mother, and she apparently regarded her parents' divorce as somewhat stigmatizing.

Therapy with Robin was surprisingly straightforward and something that every parent of a teenager has the capacity to do. It begins with affirming that the teen is indeed "experimenting" with different identities and is not yet entirely sure of just who he or she is, what she or he stands for, and where his or her life is going. This needs to be done in an understanding, sympathetic way, not a critical one. Teens need to feel that they have power over their identity, *because in fact they do.* They are no longer children whose behavior and beliefs can be effectively shaped by simple rewards and punishments.

Once this breakthrough has been made, parents then have to affirm that their teen does indeed have options, and can *choose* their identity. As I put it to Robin, "I suppose you could decide in the end that you want to be a Goth, with all that involves. On the other hand, you have personal assets and talents that can open the door to many other paths, if you so choose."

Robin and I proceeded to have an ongoing dialogue over a period of a few months. This dialogue covered pretty much all of the material in this part of the book: *who you are, what you stand for, and where you think you are going.* This is virtually the same dialogue that you as a parent can engage your teenager in. Once she or he accepts this idea of options, the risk of choosing a dysfunctional one is greatly reduced, especially if you work on building the bond between you and your teen.

In the end Robin decided to give up her flirtation with the Goths in her school. She maintained her friendships with a couple of people in that group, but gradually she returned to her former interests and friends. In large part this was due not just to therapy, but to an ongoing dialogue between Robin and Karen that paralleled Robin's talks with me.

Rather than panicking, or trying to force Robin to change by criticizing her choices, Karen took the tack recommended here: to treat adolescents with respect, including respecting their right to form an identity. At the same time Karen worked to implement as many of the ideas presented in this part of the book as possible. She staunchly maintained her position, which was that her daughter was blessed with many personal assets and had a wide range of alternative identities (and futures) that she could pursue.

Summing Up

Divorcing parents may not be in a position to offer their teenage children any guarantee that divorce will not affect them. At the same time they need to be aware that to the extent that their own future appears uncertain, that uncertainty will be amplified when viewed through the eyes of teens. This need not be cause for panic, much less despair; rather, it is a call to parents to not ignore this, to engage their teens in an ongoing dialogue, and to remember to "keep the door open" when it comes to what the future may hold.

Conclusion

This book has been designed to serve as a road map that helps you and your child weather the storm of a crisis with utmost resilience. It is a guide to keeping your child on a healthy developmental track through the three crucial years ahead. While not necessarily a bowl of cherries, hopefully there will be some good times during these years. If you follow the guidelines provided here there is a very good chance that the bond between you and your child will be stronger at the end of these three years. At the same time there is every reason to believe that your child can emerge at the end of this crisis more resilient and self-confident than he or she was before it all began.

Of course, the joys and travails of parenting will not end at the close of the three years that are the focus of this book. However, having seen your child through these times you can at least feel confident that no matter what challenges lie ahead, together you and your child can live by the motto: *We can do this!*

Chapter Notes

Note to the Reader: These notes are provided for those who are interested in learning more about the topic covered in this book. In each case, the references provided will in turn lead you to further resources in the event you are interested in pursuing a specific subject.

Introduction: The Three Crucial Years:
What Parents Need to Know about Children and Divorce

Two very influential books that initially shaped many people's views regarding the effects of divorce on children were:

Surviving the Breakup: How Children and Parents Cope with Divorce, by Judith Wallerstein and Joan Kelly, published by Basic Books, 1996.
The Unexpected Legacy of Divorce: A 25 Year Landmark Study, also by Wallerstein and Kelly, published by Hyperion, 2000.

These researchers are to be credited with making the first systematic effort to collect and report on information bearing on the question of how divorce affects children. They reported that these effects tend to be both negative and long lasting.

As important as these early studies were, they also had significant limitations that bear on their conclusions. First, they are based on a very small sample of children (sixty children took part in the study), all of whom lived in an affluent California community. It is questionable whether this sample is representative of all children of divorce. Second, the results were based solely on information obtained through interviews, as opposed to objective measures such as psychological tests and school grades. Lastly, these researchers did not include a sample of children from families in which the parents did not divorce, therefore making it difficult to determine how the children of divorce fared in comparison to children from "intact" families.

In the intervening years researchers have been able to conduct studies that correct for the above limitations. These researchers have been able to follow large numbers of children over a period of years. These samples are much more representative of all children of divorce. The researchers also complemented data obtained from interviews with objective data such as achievement test results, and tests measuring anxiety, depression, and so on. Finally, they have been able to compare children of divorce to children from intact families. Two such major studies are:

For Better or for Worse: Divorce Reconsidered, by E. Mavis Hetherington, published by W.W. Norton, 2003.
"National Education Longitudinal Study," by Yongmin Sun, reported in the *Journal of Marriage and Family,* May 2001.

It is the data reported by these two large-scale longitudinal studies that form the basis of "The Three Crucial Years." These studies strongly suggest that the majority of children—75 percent—emerge from a divorce psychologically, socially, and academically unscathed. It is the remaining 25 percent, and specifically how parents can help them avoid negative consequences, that are the focus of this book.

Chapter 2: Talking to Children about Divorce

The classic work on the stages of grief was first published by Elisabeth Kubler-Ross in 1976, but there is a newer edition: *On Death and Dying,* published by Scribner Classics, 1997.

Chapter 4: Shared Parenting: The New Look in Child Custody

Two very different references shed important light on how sharing child-rearing responsibilities can (and cannot) work well. The first is:

Halving It All: How Equally Shared Parenting Works, by Francine Deutsch, published by Harvard University Press, 1999. This researcher followed 88 couples who were *not* divorced but who shared parenting responsibilities in one of the following divided way: fifty-fifty (equally shared); sixty-forty (with one parent doing somewhat more than the other); seventy-five–twenty-five (where one parent does most of the parenting); and alternative shifts (where each parent does all the parenting in turn). The gist of the findings is that shared parenting in all of these forms *can* work but its effectiveness depends on both parents being committed to doing their share in each case. This book can be instructive to divorcing parents because it shows that shared parenting can work but only if the divorcing parents are equally committed to doing what is necessary to make it work.

In contrast to the above is the following study of divorced parents who engaged in shared parenting arrangements:

"Shared Parenting Agreements After Marital Separation: The Roles of Empathy and Narcissism," by M. Ehrenberg, M. Hunter, and M, Elterman, published in the *Journal of Consulting and Clinical Psychology*, 1996 (vol. 64, number 4). The researchers compared 16 couples who were able to successfully maintain a cooperative shared parenting plan to 16 couples who had unsuccessful shared parenting agreements, and found that the latter disagreed substantially on many parenting issues. They also found that the latter group of parents as a whole was more narcissistic, less able to take another's perspective, and less concerned about the needs and feelings of others. Clearly, these results suggest that shared parenting may not be in the best interest of all children. Some parents may need to work on taking into account the needs and feelings of others at times if their goal is to see to it that their children grow into healthy, happy adults who are capable of sustaining fulfilling relationships.

Chapter 5: New Beginnings

It is highly recommended that divorced parents who are contemplating combining two families into one blended family start reading about the issues they are likely to face, as well as ways of approaching these issues, ahead of time. The following websites offer free and useful tips on "blending." I would recommend that prospective partners visit these sites, read what some of the articles have to say, and then discuss these issues in order to come to a tentative consensus on how they will approach their and their children's new beginning.

- www.parenting.families.com: Offers a monthly newsletter that focuses on tips for blending. These tips for creating a functional, harmonious step-family are concrete and easy to follow.
- www.helpguide.org: Based on statistics showing that at least one-third of all children in the United States will be part of a stepfamily before they reach eighteen, this website is dedicated to guiding parents through the process of establishing a stepfamily.

- www.blended-families.com: This website offers a "Need help right now?" feature that allows browsers to ask specific questions. It also features articles by professionals on topics relevant to establishing a stepfamily, such as how to handle weddings.

Chapter 6: How "Resilient" Are You?

The concept of resilience was first studied in connection with corporate executives. All of these individuals could be considered to be under significant chronic stress, as they are required to make critical decisions on a day-to-day basis. Researchers were able to identify personality differences between two groups of executives: those whose physical and mental health was relatively unaffected by the exposure to chronic stress versus those whose health suffered as a result of chronic stress. They labeled the former group "hardy" executives. This research is described in detail in the following book:

The Hardy Executive: Health under Stress, by Salvatore Maddi and Suzanne Kobasa, published by Irwin Professional Publications, 1984.

Based on these initial studies with executives, the concept of hardiness—also known as *resilience*—has been extended to children and families. The information presented here has been distilled from all of this work. For more detailed information on resilience in children and families, refer to:

Resilience in Children, Families, and Communities, by Ray Peters, Bonnie Ross Leadbeater, and Robert McMahon, published by Springer, 2005.

Chapter 7: Your Emotional Health and Your Child

Researchers have found that the overall psychological adjustment of parents plays a significant role in how well children will adapt following divorce. Of a total of 15 studies that examined this issue, 13 studies found that there was a positive relationship between the mental health of divorcing parents and their children's mental health. These studies have been reported primarily in the professional literature. For those interested, refer to the following:

"Parental Divorce and the Well-Being of Children: A Meta-Analysis," by P. Amato and B. Keith, published in *Psychological Bulletin,* 1991 (vol. 110, pages 26-46).

"Children and Divorce in the 1990s: An Update of the Amato and Keith Meta-Analysis," by P. Amato, published in the *Journal of Family Psychology*, 2001 (vol. 15, pages 355-370).

The tests of anxiety and depression used in this book are based on diagnostic criteria used by mental health professionals to assess these issues. They are included here as guidelines only, not as definitive diagnostic tests. The higher a reader scores on one or more of these tests, the more strongly they are encouraged to consult with their physician or a mental health professional to clarify the extent to which anxiety or depression requires professional intervention.

Chapter 8: How Balanced is Your Lifestyle?

The material in this chapter relates to the material in Chapter 6, on your emotional health, as balancing one's lifestyle is one approach to managing anxiety or depression. The Mental Health Foundation, located in Great Britain, defines "lifestyle balance" as the way that an individual combines work with the other areas of life, such as childcare and socializing. The Foundation argues that the increased work hours typical in today's developed countries have significant and negative effects on workers' mental well-being. It conducted a survey of 577 working men and women, and found that 27 percent reported feeling depressed when forced to work longer than normal hours; 34 percent reported feeling anxious; and 58 percent reported feeling irritable. These effects have obvious implications for divorcing parents, whose life are often thrown seriously out of balance. For more information, contact the Foundation at: www.mentalhealth. org/uk/.

The guidelines presented in this chapter point readers toward restoring balance in their lifestyles. Some individuals choose to hire professional "life coaches" to help them do this. However, aside from the advice offered here, some free materials on how to better balance your lifestyle can be obtained by visiting the following websites:

- www.smokefree.gov/pubs: This is a service offered by the federal government for people who wish to stop smoking. However, it offers advice that is relevant to anyone who seeks a better balance in their lifestyle in order to improve their physical and mental health.
- www.hsrcenter.ucla.edu: This is a service offered by the University of California, Los Angeles Health Services Resource Center and includes free educational materials.

Chapter 9: Healthy versus Unhealthy Ways of Relieving Your Stress

The National Institute on Drug Abuse (NIDA) has published a special report on stress and drug abuse. It can be obtained through the NIDA website: www.drugabuse.gov/stressanddrugabuse.html. This report underscores the connection between stress and substance abuse, including alcohol and drugs.

Those who wish to contact a professional for an assessment of their use of alcohol or drugs, or to find treatment resources that is convenient to them, can identify such resources by visiting http://samhsa.gov and then clicking on the "I need help with" tab. This government database is free and confidential.

Another useful resource is the official website of Alcoholics Anonymous (AA) at www.aa.org. Its home page includes tabs that can be clicked to answer such questions as "*Is AA for you*" and "*How to Find AA Meetings.*" You can also order official AA books and pamphlets through this website.

Chapter 10: Separation and Attachment

The classic research on attachment was conducted and reported by the developmental psychologists John Bowlby and Mary D. Salter Ainsworth. Although directed primarily at professionals, their books and work is enlightening. For those who are interested, these works may be found at your local library through inter-library loan request. Two that are recommended are:

A Secure Base: Parent–Child Attachment and Healthy Human Development, by John Bowlby, published by Basic Books, 1990.
Patterns of Attachment: A Psychological Study of the Strange Situation, by Mary D. Salter Ainsworth, Mary Blehar, Everett Walters, and Sally Wall, published by Lawrence Erlbaum, 1979.

More recent research even more strongly supports the idea that problems in parent–child attachment can have dire consequences. The ongoing Adverse Childhood Experiences (ACE) study has examined more than 17,000 individuals, a cross-section of middle-class Americans. It surveyed this large sample to determine how many of these individuals had experienced one or more of the following during childhood:

- Abuse: emotional, physical, sexual abuse.

- Family dysfunction: spouse abuse, parental alcoholism or drug addiction, parent incarceration, or a chronically depressed or frequently hospitalized parent.
- Neglect: physical or emotional.

Essentially, the more of the above a person reports having experienced, the higher the ACE score. If we assume that any of the above has a negative impact on the parent–child bond, then the results of the ACE study should send up a big red flag. The researchers found a strong correlation between an individual's ACE score and the likelihood that they will later suffer from one or more of the following:

- Psychiatric disorders, especially depression, including suicidal thoughts and actions.
- Alcoholism, drug addiction, and smoking.
- Obesity and heart disease.

Readers who may wish to read about the ACE study and its startling results, it is reported in the following book:

The Hidden Epidemic: The Impact of Early Life Trauma on Health and Disease, edited by R. Lanius and E. Vermetten, published by Cambridge University Press, 2009.

Chapter 11: The Need for Exploration

If you are interested in reading more about exploration and early childhood development, the following books are very informative:

Birth to Three, by T. Berry Brazelton and Joshua D. Sparrow, published by Da Capo Press, 2006.

The earlier version of Dr. Brazelton's book has been a mainstay for parents and pediatricians for a generation. It is filled with useful information and advice.

The developmental psychologist Jean Piaget was famous for the way he was able to translate his detailed observations of his own and others' children as they developed and describe the stages through which development progresses, as well as the way young children begin to explore the world. His work is nicely summarized in the following book:

A Piaget Primer: How a Child Thinks, by Dorothy Singer and Tracey Revenson, published by International Universities Press, 1998.

Chapter 12: Divorce and Insecurity

Researchers at Notre Dame University and Catholic University of America studied 226 parents and their children aged nine to eighteen. They measured the degree to which the parents engaged in conflict, as well as the degree of anxiety in their children, and found that emotional insecurity in these children was clearly correlated with the extent to which their parents engaged in conflict.

In a second study, these same researchers assessed 232 parents and their even younger children and found similar results. These studies have clear implications for parents whose marriages are experiencing conflict, especially intense and/or frequent conflict.

For those who are interested, these studies were published in the following professional journal:

"Interparental Discord and Child Adjustment: Prospective Investigations of Emotional Security as an Explanatory Mechanism," by Mark Cummings, published in *Child Development*, 2006 (vol. 7, issue 1).

Chapter 13: Building and Maintaining a Support Network

In addition to the support network that is described in this chapter, divorcing parents may wish to reach out to others via the Internet. They can locate a variety of support groups for single parents by going to a search engine and typing in: "single parent support groups." This search will provide a wide range of resources to find support groups, which can be useful for discussing particular issues, getting advice from other single parents, or simply as venues for venting frustrations.

Strongly recommended is the following:

It Takes a Village and Other Lessons Children Teach Us, by Hillary Rodham Clinton, published by Simon & Schuster, 1996.

Chapter 14: Guiding Your Child toward Healthy Peer Groups

A lot of research has been conducted on the subject of how peer groups influence adolescent behavior. This focus of research may reflect the popular notion that the peer group influences teens more than it influences younger children. However, the position taken in this book is that divorcing parents are wise to try to steer even young children toward peer groups that parents regard as healthy or positive, rather than waiting until adolescence in order to do this.

The studies cited below illustrate how influential the peer group can be. They show that peers can exert a powerful influence on behaviors ranging from academic motivation to aggression to risk-taking behaviors.

Center for Research on Education, Diversity, and Excellence, University of California Berkeley. Visit the website www.crede.berkeley. edu for a summary of the work of this organization, which has found, among things, that teens can be influenced by their peer group to *not* do well in school. This has significant implications for parents who may see their child drifting toward a peer group that is dominated by under-achievers.

Wendy Ellis and Lynne Zarbatany report in their article in the July 2007 issue of the journal *Child Development* (vol. 78, issue 4) that the peer group can influence aggressive behavior, and that this effect is stronger the more central or "visible" a child is in that peer group (as opposed those considered "fringe" members).

Michael Keren and Ben-Zur Hasida report that, in their study of 269 Israeli teens, risk-taking behavior was heavily influenced by the peer group, especially for males. Their article appeared in the February 2007 *Journal of Adolescence* (vol. 30, issue 1).

Chapter 15: The Importance of Structure, Predictability, and Routine

Suggested further reading for those who are interested in the relationship between family structure and children's emotional health and well-being:

"Family Structure and Children's Health and Well-Being: Data From the 1988 National Health Interview," by Deborah Dawson, published in the *Journal of Marriage and the Family,* 1991.
Balancing Family and Work, by Toni Schindler Zimmerman, published by Haworth Press, 2002.

Although written for family therapists, this book contains much useful information that bears on the issue of creating order and balance in family life in order to help children stay on a healthy developmental track.

Chapter 16: Direction and Discipline

Parents seeking advice and support regarding direction and discipline can find much useful information by visiting any or all of the following websites:

- www.keepkidshealthy.com: This website describes itself as a pediatrician's guide to child health and safety.
- www.cfw.tufts.edu: A website sponsored by Tufts University that features advice and articles on a range of topics, including discipline.
- www.positivediscipline.com: This website, for teachers as well as parents, is very helpful and informative.
- www.naturalfamilyonline.com: This is a commercial website that offers support and tips on parenting, including discipline.

In addition to the above, the American Academy of Pediatrics offers a free publication titled *Guidance for Effective Discipline.* This guide was written by the Academy's Committee on Psychosocial Aspects of Child and Family Health and it is available through the following Web address: www. hhhp/aappolicy.aappublications.org/.

Chapter 17: Tantrums and Oppositional Behavior

In addition to the guidance provided here, parents faced with oppositional behavior and or temper tantrums can access additional tips and information by visiting the American Academy of Child and Adolescent Psychiatry-sponsored website www.aacap.org/cs/root/facts_for_families.

Chapter 18: School and Social Phobia

Additional support for, as well as information and advice on, dealing with school phobia is available to parents through www.phobics-awareness.org. This is a free, global help and support community. It is useful both to individuals who suffer from phobias of various kinds, and to parents who want to help a child overcome a phobia.

An informative and helpful article on school phobia, written by an experienced school psychologist, can be found by visiting www.suite101.com/. It is titled "School Phobia: Nothing to Take Lightly," by Wesley Sharpe.

Chapter 19: Guarding against Academic Failure

The below study reports on the efficacy of a method of coaching mothers and fathers in helping children with homework:

"Family Involvement with Children's Homework: An Intervention in the Middle Grades," by Sandra Balli, David Demo, and John Wedman, published by the National Council on Family Relations, April 1998 (vol. 47, number 2), available at http://www.jstor.org/stable/585619.

The below-referenced study reported that parents with a greater sense of self-efficacy were more likely to help their children with homework and also to volunteer in school. It has clear implications for parents who feel that they lack self-confidence, for this may be a factor that prevents them from getting more involved with their children's schoolwork. Self-confidence is something that ca be worked on through personal counseling. The study is:

"Explorations in Parent-School Relations," by Kathleen Hoover-Dempsey, Otto Bassler, and Jane Brissie, published in the *Journal of Educational Research*, May/June 1992 (vol. 85, number 5).

Lastly, the following study reports on how mothers' styles of coaching sons and daughters relates to those children's compliance with parental expectations, including doing homework:

"Mothers' Social Coaching, Mother-Child Relationship Style, and Children's Compliance: Is the Medium the Message?," by Jacquelyn Mize and Gregory Pettil, published in *Child Development*, April 1997 (vol. 68, number 2).

Chapter 20: Alcohol and Drugs

To find out more about the effects of alcohol on health, visit the National Institute on Alcohol Abuse and Alcoholism website at www.niaaa.nih.gov/.

An informative review of the effects of alcohol on health is: "Alcohol-Related Morbidity and Mortality," by J. Rehm, G. Gmel, C. Sempos, and M. Trevisan, M.

Part Five: Chapters 21 to 24

These chapters describe the process of identity development in adolescents. The pioneering work in this area was done by developmental psychologist Erik H. Erikson and described in the following books:

Identity: Youth and Crisis, by Erik H. Erikson, published by W.W. Norton
   in an updated edition in 1994.
Childhood and Society, by Erik H. Erikson, also published in an updated edition by Vintage Books in 1995.

Erikson's emphasis on the importance of identity development is summarized succinctly in the following sentence from *Identity: Youth and Crisis:*
"In the social jungle of human existence there can be no feeling of being
alive without a sense of identity." Readers interested in further exploring
the subject of identity development are encouraged to read Dr. Erikson's
books.

In addition, this author has written a book on identity development in
teens:

The Identity Trap: Saving Our Teens from Themselves, by Joseph Nowinski,
   published by Amacom Books, 2007.

This book offers parents specific advice on steering their teens toward
healthy, productive identities.

Finally, an excellent example of how identity is influenced by relationships is to be found in the story of Malcolm X:

The Autobiography of Malcolm X, by Malcolm X and Alex Haley, published
   by Penguin Classics, 2001.

About the Author

Joseph Nowinski, Ph.D. has over 25 years experience counseling individuals, couples, and families, many of whom have had to negotiate the issues described in this book. Dr. Nowinski's other books include *The Tender Heart: Conquering Your Insecurity; Six Questions that Can Change Your Life;* and *The Identity Trap: Saving Our Teens from Themselves,* which won a 2008 Silver Nautilus Book Award in the Parenting category. He lives with his family in Tolland, Connecticut. For further information visit www.josephnowinski.com.

Index